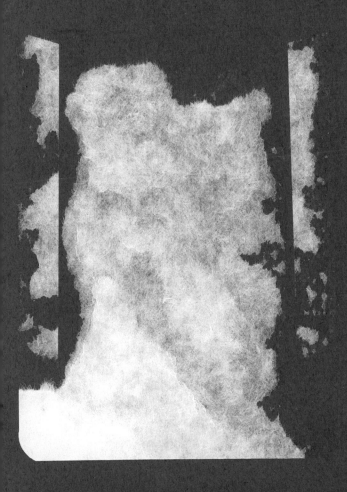

Allen Mandelbaum

CHELMAXIOMS:

the Maxims · Axioms · Maxioms

of Chelm

DAVID R. GODINE
PUBLISHER · BOSTON

in association with
The Jewish Publication Society of America
PHILADELPHIA

ACKNOWLEDGMENTS

The "Preface of the Hoarse Savant" and Maxioms 1 through 16 of the Third Finding first appeared in *The Denver Quarterly*; the five "Gatesongs," in *Living Hand*; "The Song of Offspring" from the Sixth Finding, in *Poetry*; Maxiom 6 of the Fourth Finding (as "The Phantom Chant") and "The Ayre of If" from the Sixth Finding, in *The Beloit Poetry Journal*. "The Chant of the Hoarse Savant" in the Sixth Finding alters—and supplants— "Time Squared," which appeared in *Journeyman*, Schocken Books, 1967.

David R. Godine · Publisher
306 DARTMOUTH STREET, BOSTON, MASSACHUSETTS 02116

ISBN 0-87923-214-5
LCC 77-78398

First Printing: September 1977
PRINTED IN THE UNITED STATES OF AMERICA

Other books by Allen Mandelbaum

POETRY
Journeyman, 1967
Leaves of Absence, 1976

VERSE TRANSLATIONS
Life of a Man by Giuseppe Ungaretti, 1958
Selected Writings of Salvatore Quasimodo, 1960
The Aeneid of Virgil, 1972 (National Book Award, 1973)
Selected Poems of Giuseppe Ungaretti, 1975
The Inferno of Dante (forthcoming)

THE MAXIOMS are inscribed: to the memory of my father, Albert Naphtali; to the text, talk, and companionship of the *Kantkreis*; and to Margherita, who watched over the making of the major portion of the Maxioms in Orta S. Giulio and on the Rue d'Assas from July 1972 to the following summer. ⁌ I am grateful indeed to Monika Forndran and Giselle Neuschloss of the Graduate Center of the City University of New York for their help in work on the Scoriae; to Holly Hall of the Rare Book Room of Olin Library at Washington University in St. Louis; and, finally, to Dr. Menachem Schmelzer, Chief Librarian of the Jewish Theological Seminary.

CONTENTS

꙳

CHELMAXIOMS

And when
he dreams he does not want to write,
he does not have the power to dream
he wants to write; and when he dreams
he wants to write, he does not have
the power to dream he does not want
to write.

The Preface of
THE HOARSE SAVANT

The hoarse savant—begetter and bequeather of this preface to the Six Findings of CHELMAXIOMS—*is surely a son of Chelm. But which of the eleven tribes (the legalists, the spinozists, the ararites, the pindarites, the agonists, the kabalists, the tortoisists, the analogists, the metamorphosists, the ecclesiastesists, or—those who fed on likelihood and thus made do with meagerness—the wise) can claim him? Indeed, did he belong to one, to some, to all, to none? Of that I have—as yet—received no certain knowledge.*

Some were born into Chelm. Some found it. Some refound it.

Chelm is the Diaspora writ large—or more precisely, the second Diaspora, for Babylonia saw the first but engendered no Chelm.

Chelm is the Diaspora writ small, but nurtured in the narrow compass of its walls by the scoriae, residues, sediments of all the encounters of the Jew in exile: his meeting with Greece (witness the pindarites), his second meeting with Babylonia (witness Sura and Pumbeditha and Saadya), his finding of Spain and of France, of Portugal, of Holland, of Germany, of Italy, of Russia, of the cultures of the Logos, of the Cross, of Islam (or better, Islams—how various is the Mohammedan itinerary), and of the flame—at once an *ignis fatuus* and an endless holy fire—of the Emancipation. And of the of.

[xv]

By Chelm I do not mean—of course—the counterfeit, usurping Chelm of Yiddish folklore, the Chelm that finds its careful Hebrew chronicler in the *Sefer ha-Bedicha*, the Chelm that is so derivative of—so indebted for its humor to—early German lumpen humor, the Chelm that wanton Smyrna may ape with countermaxioms.

By Chelm I mean the *echt* Chelm, the meandering Chelm of the maxioms, which follow the non sequiturs—yet arabesque—of talk of talk and talk of text, which mime the riverlike careers of the Oral Law and the Written Law but carry a cargo of alegalities—the divagations, digressions, the discreet and indiscreet parentheses native to talmudic/midrashic exegesis. Indeed, if the Talmud already has two redactions—Jerusalem's and Babylon's—why not, the maxioms ask, a third?

Yet, like the false Chelm, the *echt* Chelm also has its undertow of absurdity: the absurdity inherent in analogical and numerological revery—eleven tribes, eleven quays, six findings, five gates, five cesurasongs, two tutelary birds, two tutelary trees, two tutelary shapes (the equilateral rhombus, the more recalcitrant rhomboid)—talismans that proliferate in nights at the total table (for it was at the total table that the Chelm Sanhedrin met, as we shall see, on every even day except when even fell on odd because of overwhelming restlessness). The absurdity inherent in too tenacious lust for the Absolute.

And the perfect woman, pensive distant offspring of the woman/women of the Song of Songs (a work that entered the canon clandestinely, by way of the Gate of Phantom, while she entered by way of the Gate of the Event), is only too aware of the self-aggrandizing, self-wounding savant-erie of those absurdities.

That province, that village of the mind which draws on—and comprehends—such disparate sites and times of Exile has *some* relation to Orta S. Giulio. For it was on the Lake of Orta that, after the destruction of Chelm in World War II, I survived long enough, the only Jew (the epigraph to Mario Levi and his son, inscribed in memorial stone on a wall a brief walk away from the Piazza Ragazzoni, records the deportation of the only Jews to precede me), to record what I could of the maxioms. And no telling can fully deny the place in which it is told (or its time—and Maxiom Eleven of the Fifth Finding echoes the Czech events of August 1968).

I spoke of the destruction of Chelm. That destruction seals a sense of absence into the Hebrew month of Heshvan, the autumnal month called *"mar"* Heshvan, "bitter" Heshvan, because no feast days fall within its span. But even the Heshvan of deprivation, the void in the calendar, cannot obliterate the plentitude of that Exile, the seldom silenced talk that lies behind these maxioms: cantilena, lied, song, sonatina, chant.

The chanter is not an historian, but his voice begins where the historian's begins.

He breathes in time.

He too must come to terms with termini.

He too seeks the fleeting Gates of Talk, of Text, of Man, of Phantom, of the Event.

Aloud.

GATESONGS
for the five entryways to Chelm

1

The walker walks along woodways.
The trunks are granite, taupe, black.

The walker comes from Ararat.
He leans against a granite trunk.

The journey here has often veered.
The tree beyond is eucalyptus.

There the tacit forest ends.

The woodway vanishes in path
that wanders south and sinuous
across a plain. He hesitates.

The plain is watched by sinuate
foothills that alter as he walks:

their ridges so entwine, no gloss—
by patient sun or patient dusk—
can ever find their final lines.

Eleven leagues—and he can see
a lake, an island in the lake.

In leaf, along the lakeside quays:
eleven gestruemias.

He lingers under each: he reads
the light that lives
beneath their leaves.

He hears a swaying of reeds.
Of parts of speech.

He comes from distant Ararat.
That flood is past.

He sees the walls, the gates
of Chelm.

He waits.

2

He waits before the walls of Chelm,
that shelter men and maxioms;
he has abandoned coarse canards,

deriding words he may have heard
from babblers who belittled or
maligned the meditative sons

of Chelm with fables fouler far
than cellar stews of Smyrna are
(or dens along the Bosphorus),

with lies that touch no fault of flesh
but what is still more frail in us—
the work of word as witness.

And—even as the one who waits
before the five and patient gates—
may all who did not question when

men said the alleyways of Chelm
contained more fools than all the plains
that lead to Chelm and back again—

forget that lying legend hatched
by charlatans with yataghans.

Remember: malice is the spawn
of cunning countermaxioms.

3

Within the alleyways of Chelm
there dwell revehent time as well
as time that is to be revealed;

and there, by lantern light and when
that lantern light was spent, the un-
remitting men of Chelm—again,

again—revised the maxioms
that either time consigned to them,
but seldom sent their testament

across the final Gate of Text—
as if finality might mean
the end of Chelm and of its men.

What lived and lied outside the walls
were scumbled words, half-heard and dark,
and unilluminated scrawls

and fragments free to sham as wholes
when lids had never opened on
the eucalyptus gates of Chelm

or on the light of lakeside quays
(where talk of men and waves and reeds
would often mingle in one lied),

when eyes had never known the square
(whose only fountain blessed the air
with cool cadenzas in midsummer)

and lacked the pensive alphabet,
the *Vast and Versal Lexicon*,
the only vision that can span

the meanings of the men and when
the perfect woman came to Chelm.

4

The eucalyptus gates of Chelm
had risen well before the walls.

There were the gates.
That was all.

There were the gates.
There was no place.

The walls were built in Exile.

Beneath the patient foothills,
upon the plain of Exile
the walls of Chelm became.

Without the stones of Exile
the walls would still await.

Within the one horizon
no path would interrupt
the plain or wander north
to find itself woodway.

The lake would shelter herons
and cranes and share the lied
of waves and reeds but not
of men along the quays.

Exile had found the site.

Exile gave Chelm to light.

5

Woodways. Plain. Horizon. Wall.
The walker walks within recall.

The Gate of Talk.
The Gate of Text.

The walker comes from Ararat.
(Ararat can flood again.)

The walker in recall has drawn
closer.

The Gate of Man.
The Gate of Phantom.

He sees the total table.
He hears the canticle.

The total table has
the scent of eucalyptus.

The canticle is fragile.

It says
the table is a rhombus.

It says a vase was meant
to be on the total table.

It says
there is a Gate of the Event.

To near is not to enter;
to enter, not to know.

To know is not to be.
But speech is touch,

is wound, caress, is
revery of entry.

THE FIRST FINDING
of maxims/maxioms/axioms

כנור

היה תלוי

למעלה ממיתתו

של דוד וכיון שהגיע

חצות לילה בא רוח צפונית

ומנשבת בו ומנגן

מאליו

1

The men of Chelm do not despair:
they lift their lances in the air
and leave them there.

2

The men of Chelm remember:
who raises maxioms in air
must never wave them.

3

The men of Chelm are not at all unstable.

First they build themselves a total table:
a robust rhombus sawed from eucalyptus
their axes felled in the elusive forests
eleven leagues beyond the lake of Chelm,
just where Auriga rises in the autumn.

This total table serves intensive uses:
on this, they set their massive axioms;
at this, they study, revery, sleep, and eat—
until it loses all of its two feet.

And then they wait upon the floor
for more

axioms.

4

The carpenters of total tables
tremble at the thought of flaw;
at each evasive edge they chant
the vast and versal Chant of Awl.

They sang without a part of speech—
until they fell on two more phemes
and alternated /awl/ and /all/
and found the peace we cannot reach

when solitary song is heard
and strays without the stay of words
to places, cravings that appall
if we remember what we were

before the wordless canticle.

5

As you came from the walls of Chelm
or as you travelled toward them,
if you had met a son of Chelm
and walked and paused and shared the parts
of speech and speechlessness, the harsh-

the-hushed-the-dry-the-moist-the-rushed-
andante-lento-comatose-
the-congruous-the-disparate-
the-brusque-the-hesitant-the-hoarse-
the-wick-the-flame-the-wax-the-spent-

the-uninhabited-the-nomad-
crowded-chosen-and-rejected-
furtive-fecund-resurrected-
shimmering-debris-and-dross-
the-point-the-plane-the-cavernous-

the-pulp-the-pit-the-ripe-the-raw-
the-gnawed-defaced-abashed-embraced-
the-clamorous-the-una-corda-
naked-breathless-banished-pneuma-
fluent-force-of-pharynx-flaw,

and—while you veered across the plain
and heard the daughters of the crane
vociferate in flight until
their white isosceles fell still
on reaching reeds—had asked him:

And can the azure of the maxims
reach or render the endured?

He would have said: Uneasiness
and doubt are dark and ancient;
but in the light of maxims, they—
and any body bearing them—
may touch the unprecarious.

6

But others say he would have said
that hope is harder far to bear
than doubt: beneath its weight we break
or fall—before we reach the Gates
of Talk and Text—to weariness

unless the maxims' music wakes
(even as the northwind played—
while the exhausted psalmist slept—
upon the lyre in his tent,
until it had awakened him)

us.§

7

And while you walked as one and watched
the sun, the scumbled clouds, the dusk,
or light of lucid Deneb touch
the foothills—if you asked him just
as unobtrusively as reeds
sway beyond the lakeside quays:

And why, when bearing witness, must
the maxioms desert the course
the lake of Chelm has taken—calm
midsummer flow that never bends
unless the fluent winds intend—
and wind and writhe instead and wend
as would the mad Maiandros?
Or want the way that arrows may
but end as amphisbaenas?

---

§*And some—although asymmetry
is truer to the torsion we
endure beneath the weight of hope—*

*would, even as we bend, emend
and shift us from a bias left
and center us instead—thus:*
                    us.

He then would say:
Diaspora
is still the way
of shreds and shards,
of all that frays,
discolored words,
and leaves astray,
and winds that scatter
nesting birds—

and we cannot remember
the order
of the sayings of the fathers.

8

But others
say the fathers
themselves were random, garrulous,
that Chelm was not the capital of silence,

that brevity was won but often lost again
in labyrinths, distracted paths,
and mazes mapped
in galimatias.

9

The men of Chelm
do not despair:

They lift their
lances in the air

and leave them
there.

10

Maimonides
was on his knees.

Averroes
would rather sneeze
than pray.

Spinoza prayed
another way.

All three of them
have followers
in Chelm.

11

The men of Chelm
need not contend
with three-in-one
and one-in-three:

for them
what bothered Abelard
is not hard.

12

The god of Chelm
did not descend
as bull or swan
or dove; some men
of Chelm, our ten
most intransigent
metamorphosists,

at times may tend
to mourn or miss
this—then   again
acknowledge   some
assuaging   in the
keeping   of their
women for them-
        selves.

13

The metamorphosist is most
engrossed by waves and walls
and clouds—by mottled walls
and clouds whenever scumbled
and waves when most autumnal;

when these are not at hand,
he stands astonished and
deciphers dusk on foothills,
discolored scrolls, the fall
and rise of our one fountain:

wherever shadows shift
and veer and light is born
and dies and then is scanned
again, each hieroglyph
compels the metamorphosist

as he recovers or divines
for every want an icon
and needs no rite of rhyme,
refrain, or incantation
to conjure the clandestine.

14

one breath

away from wrath

he watched

demented clouds

refuse the

lineaments

he imposed

15

But some say metamorphosists
have always gathered in their gifts
with neither fountain, wave, wall,

nor cloud nor any thing at all
to hear or touch or see when lids
are locked and one can live in null

and absence as if they were full;
for—certain harvesters have known—
the furrows of *creatio*

are endless when *ex nihilo.*

16

Yet some who stray by night insist
that, far beyond the Gate of Text,
they saw the apprehensive scrawl
a metamorphosist had scratched—
when sightless—on a grotto wall:

If only there were light enough to feel
one's way along the walls of the world, to find
the flaw the builders had not seen, to foil
the unassuageable architects, to fall
into fidelity, if there were light . . .

17

Some men of Chelm are not attached to time;
and some of them are so attached that when
it passes, unremitting trembling takes them.

Both sects sequester every hourglass
and, after emptying the avid sands,
refill the upper halves with patient rocks

that, when they find decline is difficult
through such a fragile funnel, will forgo
the fall—and wait within their stony trance

until the time has come to avalanche.

18

He may be passive,
but let him live.

19

That very man meandering north
  to meet the tacit forest,
  when he has seen the stands of dense
tree trunks and shadows so intense
  they could confound Spinoza's lens,
  will turn about and south,

and may retrace eleven leagues
  to find the light of lakeside quays
  (where pale savants can gloss the sun
until the bitter moon of Heshvan,
  summer's crescent colophon,
  ends their exegeses),

and, since the lake embraces town,
  may even wander into Chelm
  to watch the rhomboid fountain;
unless—when that inconstant man
  has gone to woods and back again—
  distraction and digression

(most frequent at the start of spring
  and at the turning of the leaves
  and just at the inditing:
wherever living, dying speak—
  across their thin parentheses—
  discreetly to each other)

do not divert him elsewhere.

20

He is digressive,
but let him live.

21

The sages sighed.
They looked again:
the Song of Songs
was in the canon.

They were wrong:
the canon should
have been within
the Song of Songs.

22

But when the winter winds had swept
the sky with anabatic clouds
deleting every star except
for lucid Deneb—one who walked
by night beyond the Gate of Talk
would ask and answer as he paused
to murmur in the winter wind:§

The Canticle of Canticles?

It is too weak a wall
and too inclined to rubble—

to shelter scroll or soul
or testament or canon

of man or perfect woman.

---

§*More certain men emend:*
  to reason in the winter wind.

23

And one who never needed more
than one benighted arbor—or

a furtive lantern, wanton fountain,
haunting paralimnion,

or unadorned *pinarium*—
before he sang the Song of Songs

(and when he chanted chanted so—
glissando serpentine vibrato

dulcet desperate disheveled
pliant fescennine rubato

diapason *recto tono*
wan decanted decrescendo

meager mendicant redundant
sham—immoderately and

in ways unknown to man) contends
that it is even frailer than

the fragile canticle of sense.

24

But those who only found their force
within the blackest reach of forest

would always wince in brusque disgust
beneath the light of lakeside quays

(where some savants would scan the sun
and softly gloss the Song of Songs)

and, having winced, would conjure us:
The canon should have been within

Ecclesiastes.

25

For some in Chelm have shunned
the versal sun and some
the path from seed to volume—

but none by way of Origen,
along the edge of yataghan.

26

The
men
of
Chelm
do
not

despair:
they
lift
their
lances
in

the
air
and
leave
them
there.

27

One hoarse savant, who always had
to free his pharynx of the phlegm
that harassed him no end in Chelm,

would cough, sough, rasp, erupt, and then
consent to let his raucous head
repose upon his beard—that read

much like a motley palimpsest
where three distracted scribes had flecked
grey, white, and russet inks—and add

this word whenever asked how certain
disconcerting, dark, or wanton
parts of speech had found the canon:

They entered through the Gate of Phantom.

28

And if you were to ask;
And why did phlegm harass?

Whenever ardent agonists
had gathered in their blackest vests
to sigh the sighs of soft respect
for any word another spoke—
until they heard that word and went—
despite the reins of reverence—
bashi-bazouk

with pararhyme and paradox
that fell like madding mamelukes
or leaped like breakneck *landsknechts*
on any uttered tenet,
on well- or one-armed sentences
or sentences defenseless, slack,
distracted, sprawling, broken-backed,

maneuvering the maxioms
and countermaxioms of Chelm
across the camps of apothegm
and dubium and scholium
and myrmidons of maxims—
and then across themselves—
in paths like boustrophedon,

in melees, waylays, forays
of epiexegeses
along the lakeside quays
(or else around the fountain—
just at the center of our square—
whose cool cadenzas in the air
have always blessed midsummer),

he never could resist
the fetish in his pharynx
that lacked a taste for silence,
and never quell the itch
that lived in all his lemmas
to touch the green dilemma
that hides behind the last:

he hurried for his blackest vest,
as bashi-bazouk as the rest.

29

The anodynic pulse that beats
from each ascending lid to each

descending lid as patient sleep
invites the cilia to meet

incites the agonist to leap.

30

The cranes,
the herons
stir their
wings then
still them,
entering the reeds.

THE FIRST FINDING NOW IS FOUND

Around the diamond border, starting from the top and going clockwise:

WHEN EACH HAS FOUND IT CANNOT REACH PEACE RETREAT: SPEECH TO MEET SILENCE ; SILENCE ; SPEECH. VIOLENCE OF SILENCE, VIOLENCE OF SPEECH:

CESURASONG ONE
for the interval between
the First and Second Findings

THE SECOND FINDING
of axioms/maxims/maxioms

דברה תורה כלשון בני אדם

1

They say
that any man who blessed
his fountain, forest, lake
but kept
his blessing back
from even one
elsewhere
could not have been from Chelm.

2

But others disagree with that:
they say that there were plutocrats
and *apparatchiks*, even rats
who, when the winter fell, grew fat
on grain and gain and others' pain.

But most of these lived in the suburbs.

3

And some have held
some men of Chelm
were even Abbevillian:

in no sense men of maxioms
but of two-edged stone axes.

4

The island in the lake of Chelm
had monsters once. They scattered them.

And now the monsters live on land:
the island in the lake of Chelm
remains the only place with none

or—when a countermaxiom
has disembarked—with one.§

5

So lucid was Saadya Gaon
that even Deneb when it shone

with all its brother stars upon
the northern paralimnion

that lines the waves of Chelm, beyond
the island, in a stillness none,

no lake or night, had ever known—
not even at the moment just

before a part of speech is glossed—
would hang its head when faced with his

clarities.

---

§*Though others would emend:*
or—when a countermaxiom
or lonely Abbevillian
would visit it—with one.

6

Yet some reject this text and say
the simile was surely not a
celebration of Saadya:

it was a singsong
dwelling on
Maimonides'

lucidities.

7

Beneath the light of lakeside quays,
where talk of men and waves and reeds
would mingle in a single lied,

to ponder dim paternities
can only serve to vex, obsess,
and even ostracizes rest:

for some allege the father
of truth is talk, while some say text;
and—quaere even more perplexed—

who must have been his mother?
Some shout that she was murmur,
some mutter she was shout;

and others say that either/or
he was stillborn without a doubt;
and some have countered: Not at all;

he certainly was twin of doubt,
but doubt was first to ferret out
and cannot be compelled—

by force or love or lentil—
to sell, bequeath, or barter
his birthright—with a brother

so harassed, haunted, pale.

8

The eucalyptus gates of Chelm
(on each evasive side that faced:
to fountain, foothills, plain, or lake)
had been inscribed with hieroglyphs.

Of these, the more elaborate
were on the Gates of Talk and Text:

the first, in high—yet indistinct—
relief; the latter, in relief
that—although low and quite discreet—
was most meticulously etched.

Some said that they were rhombic,
and some said arabesque.

Some said they were oblique
and others said direct.

Some said that they were parts of speech
and some contended: Wholes.

While others said: To face a text—
remember Ishmael.

9

Rav Ishmael had never seen the walls
of Chelm, that shelter men and maxioms;
for Chelm is, after all, the place of Exile—
its walls were won long after Ishmael.

But Ishmael would walk with Rav Akiva,
and both Akiva and Rav Ishmael
already knew the Gates of Text and Talk—
and it was there the two would always walk.

And if a gate without a wall may seem
a wounded thing, consider well the shame
of walls without a gate, and Ishmael
considered that far more lamentable.

For once, when he had walked with Rav Akiva,
and as they walked, they quarreled, Ishmael
insisted that the Torah spoke the language
of men. No tenet could have been more simple.

And yet Maimonides and—after him—
the men Maimonides had unperplexed,
because they had neglected gates and walls,
misunderstood the words of Ishmael:

they said he held that God must condescend
to those who went far lower than He went.
But all Rav Ishmael had ever meant:
Not every letter carries strict intent—

the speech of God, the speech of man, are loose;
do not use exegesis as a noose;
no maxim, axiom, maxiom, no law
must stand as if it were a gateless wall.

[37]

10

The /law/, the /wall/:
more phemes of Chelm
and not ephemeral.

11

A stranger came, a karaite:
he nested and he left by night—
and always by the Gate of Text.

He only prized the Written Word,
a single wing and much too light
for crane or son of Chelm in flight.

How less the life, how flawed the bird:
one who would rather walk
than fly—and write than talk.

12

The snow is at the Gate of Text
   and at the Gate of Talk, and yet
   with eyes intent while spine is bent
and sways within the silent hall,
   without a stove, without a glove
   to dam the damp of winter's walls,

by patient lantern light and, when
   that lantern's pallid light is spent,
   beside a rhomboid candle,
with only one companion,
   the pandect he has placed upon
   the eucalyptus lectern,

how sinuous, how various,
   his path across the provinces
   of far a fortiori,
along the passes that may twist
   but mount until they reach as if
   then plummet to imply,

when nothing stirs the evil urge
   to vagabond and ache, subvert
   within the tacit night,
and nothing can disturb or curb
   what pindarites might well have called—
   though he would not have called at all—

his long katabasis.

* * * * *

     (And into silence so intact
       he sang and sent
       without a let
       the living text:
       the harsh and soft,
       the it, the what,
       the slack, the taut,
       the may, the must,
       at once irate,
       infuriate,
       indulgent,
       mute,
       grandiloquent,
       inept,
       consummate,
       straight
       and errant,

future, past,
will send, have sent,
will mean, have meant,
testament,
fragment,
fulfillment,
present,
I think, am thought,
am doubted, doubt,
scintilla, dust,
event,
commandment,
clearing, forest,
arbor, thicket,
harbor, tempest,
trough and crest,
land's end and yet
continent,
the why, the that,
behemoth, ant,
tantamount
to keel, to mast,
to sole, to last,
to head, to hat,
to love, to threat,
to bridge, to moat,
magnanimous but
obdurate,
decisive, moot,
prolix and curt,
ambush, overt,
defiant, pliant,
thus and but,

          erect,
          recumbent,
          shame and trust,
          to shun, to want,
          a shard, complete,
          advance, retreat,
          set free and pent,
          hermetic, quite
          transparent,
          quest
          and rest,
          as if, as ought,
          the the, the nought,
          relentless yet
          compassionate
        cantilena of the Oral Law.)

* * * * *

Of course—there were sporadic coughs
    (but always his) and random barks
    of distant dogs within their dark
and, when they heard that some have held
    the morning star is Venus' self,
    the anxious amphibrachs of cocks;

and he had thought on what was not,
    the subtle force of absence,
    the craft of what is lost:
the fountain's cool cadenzas
    that always blessed midsummer
    and now were ice and silent.

But none of these—the coughs,
   the barks, the crowing cocks, the thought
   of not—could interrupt
the cantilena of the Law,
   consigned from speech to folio
   by men condemned to sleeplessness

because of their concern for us,
   their fear that we might never know
   it all—if all recall were left
to talk alone—that can digress
   and stray from canticle of sense
   to self-indulgence and abet

forgetfulness.

* * * *

And after ninety nights have passed
   with eyes intent, exhausted lamps
   or candlelight, while spine is cramped,
without a stove to save the walls—
   that wall the silent study hall—
   from all the arsenal of wiles

in the attack of winter's damp,
   that will at first insinuate
   and then assail, annihilate,
his body is a stone,
   his tendons climbed a mountain,
   descended into caverns,

his eyes may see a vision
    but not of what's before them,
    his flesh has lost its latch to bone,
his bladder seems a demijohn,
    his head—hardly a fountain
    of limpid disputation;

and yet—precisely then—
    dismaying maxioms can come,
    even as the Sabbath Queen
arrives when we are most fatigued—
    and she herself is weak and wan
    with weight of laws—to bring

transfiguring.

13

A port beyond our portulans,
a bay too brilliant for man,
where light alone can dwell:
from that elusive harbor
the Sabbath Queen sets sail

and reaches us—always as dusk
would touch the patient foothills—
some three days after she began
her journey out of speechlessness,
her pilgrimage to Chelm.

She stays a single day—until
another dusk has touched foothills.

Would she might moor for all the week
to spare herself the long fatigue
of three days journey out
and three days journey in
and the uncertain seas

and so save us
the anxiousness,
the everlasting labor,
the mourning her departure,
the six days waiting for her.

14

And once, within the tacit hall,
beside the pandects of the law,
a most persuasive kabalist
arrived with an assiduous
lantern; it was always lit
through thirteen thoughtful years

(much like the span that Luria
had spent on the alluvial
shoreline of the silent Nile—
when even night could never still
the sun that spoke within his will
until the parts of speech were whole).

And some have said his logogriphs
were often too elusive.

But others have contended: If
they veiled the sign, they let it live.

15

Still others chant that, when he left,
a chariot was sent for him:
no stallions, just two cherubin
conversing in
an Aramaic sweeter far—
and with more penetrating sense—
than anything Safed had uttered.

They waited at the Gate of Text
and at the Gate of Talk.

They waited. But he did not come.

For thirteen nights they waited. Then
they found him at the Gate of Phantom.

And in the interval between
arrival and departure,
they murmured—but they did not seem.

16

Why are there two redactions:
Jerusalem and Babylon?

To teach us that there is not one—
and, given two, that there is room

for more: for Chelm, for maxioms.

17

The way from Pumbeditha back
to Sura and from Sura back
to Pumbeditha always passed
through Chelm. That way was not direct.

Neither was Sinai.

18

The cranes
and herons
never stay
beyond the
second day
of Heshvan

and leave
the plain
and reeds
in flight
that some
have said

is frequently deflected.

THE SECOND FINDING NOW IS FOUND

CESURASONG TWO

for the interval between
the Second and Third Findings

> He
> often
> walked
> without
> a part of
> speech: a hand
> without a branch.

THE THIRD FINDING
of axioms/maxioms/maxims

כי אס לבינה תקלא

1

We sent a very pensive mission out
from Chelm for the ascent of Ararat.

But when they passed Salonika and Smyrna
and came to camp in arid Anatolia,
they found the fluent name had suffered change,
that Ararat was only Agri Dagi.

And five impatient men turned back again,
convinced the shift had undermined and meant
no man can stand upon that apogee;

the other five kept pressing on—the same
maintained the mass of mountains was more constant
than veering vowels and landslide consonants.

And yet the newer name darkened their path:
despite their search in five, they found no past.

2

Eleven Songs of Ararat
were sung by saddened ararites
on their return—and some allege
that they were long and intricate—
but all that we have left is one
graffito at the fountain's edge:

mountain

with
  neither
   sea
    lake
     river
      torrent
       cloud
        rain
         estuary

        skeleton

3

However arid,

Ararats
of talk
or text

can flood:
one cloud—

Izmir may
veer then
disappear
among the
souks of
Smyrna;

Maiandros
seeks to
wend but
ends in
bends of
Menderes;

the truth
descends
to stews
of thrut;

and doubt
is thrust—
and must
corrupt—
among the
sunless
dens of dobut.

Some die
to keep
an Agri
Dagi dry.

4

They journeyed out, they journeyed back;
but five who searched at Ararat
found nothing there and nothing less—

on their return—than they had left:
all our antiquities were where
they were before departure.

We had Spinoza's lens.
We had the wounded Underwood
that Osip Mandelstam had used

when, in a disconcerting song,
the visitor from Petrograd
said any sonatina man had

ever typed upon its keys
could only mime a music
more rich than that machine's.

We had what some had called the cap
the Besht had worn when he had danced
upon the cold Carpathians.

But we had nothing Noahide
and even more distressing lacks—
great rents in time, unoccupied.

And yet we seldom seem to miss more relics.
And some have long asserted: Absence lives.

5

The summer of the ararites'
return—the most diluvian
the plain of Chelm had ever known:
the catabatic winds had brought
three months of rain. And it remained.

The alleyways, the square, the men
were more morose than random dogs
on nights deprived of Deneb's light,
or foothills in the vise of fog,
or text when trapped in clouds of gloss.

And yet the gestruemias
towered undismayed:

along the lakeside quays,
they flowered forty days,

converting that dull element—
the rain of Chelm—to waves

of mauve exuberance.

6

That summer long
the lizards of Chelm
avoided the sun.

Though some would add:
Chelm had not had
sun that summer long.

That summer done,
the lizards left for Agrigentum.

7

We never heard if they arrived.

Even as far
back as Pindar
all word between
the gates of Chelm—
that may have lived millennia
before the walls had risen—
and plain of Agrigentum
was slow, uncertain, often
unintelligible.

Some say that situation will grow better.

But others say a common alphabet
will only net
the parts of speech we want to throw away.

In any case the lizards may
be lost.

8

In speaking of the lizards, we forgot
those men of Chelm who got their citrons not
from Galilee by way of Smyrna but—
although that route was far more intricate
and crossed an alp more harsh than Ararat—
from Agrigentum for the Feast of Harvest.

And they were known as pindarites, a sect
that always sang dismaying psalms; they said
that, though they seldom understood the words,
as long as they had breath enough and odes,
they never would neglect those cryptic texts:
the meters passed all measures mortals heard.

9

Some leagues beyond the lake of
Chelm, within a clearing which
had won a parallelogram of sun
from the tenacious forests, the
pindarites long since inscribed
as wallwords on a hunting lodge
they built of eucalyptus logs—
a lodge where what they hunted
was rhombus: TO THE MAKER OF
THE FIRST ARROW/ *You will find
symmetry——or will go hungry.*

10

How passionately pindarites have wished
   that Oedipus had saved his sight for this
   or else had heard it while there still was time
   to find that kinship need not be malign
(the text is tractate *Blessings*, as you know,
   on Folio Fifty-seven, on the recto;
   though some mistake the number of the line):

The man who dreams of sleeping with his mother—
   and count on this as on a trusted father—
   will wake to understanding that is keener,
   for understanding bears the name of mother;
and if he dreams of sleeping with his sister,
   he can rely on finding wisdom's weather,
   that is, the air of vast and versal summer.

(They do not dwell on fathering a brother
   or else a nephew for one's self and sister,
   but even such oneirics might not bother
   the exegetes' benign barometer;
indeed the elders always seem to augur
   benevolence for minds that dream of matter
   that can but knit the clan and kith together.)

11

But he who dreams of sleeping with his wife
has paradise.

12

When every man was Schliemann
   and ruins were the rage,
   six hoarse savants encouraged
the burrowing of Chelm
   (no savant touched the ground
   and yet they showed us where
to start: the rhomboid fountain
   within our rhomboid square),
   stupendous excavations
somewhat like those at Paestum
   although we had no shovels—
   and not one Doric temple
to spur our expectations
   before we even had begun
   to overturn the fountain

(yet pindarites did tremble
   and shake at any shard
   we found in any clod;
and as the soil collapsed,
   they blessed the burrowing
   of Chelm with amphibrachs—
and even sang one paean
   that would have made Poseidon
   leave the sea to listen—
had he not been uncertain,
   not feared for some confusion
   in any formal welcome
that Chelm might offer him—
   one come as inundation
   within our lonely pantheon).

We dug from Chelm above
   and found more Chelm below
   as far as psalms can go
and only can conjecture
   that even at the center
   our findings would not alter
(and understand that once
   a Tuscan met with much
   the very same results,
although that Tuscan dug
   some hundred cantos up
   and down with sharper tercets
than any man has found
   to probe the shifting ground
   where any fountain stands).

13

A pindarite,
concerned that one
among the ararites might be
a victim of Mnemosyne,
along the unobtrusive wall—
where they were sure to walk—
had scrawled
in cautionary majuscules
and modest semi-uncials:

HAVING COMMITTED ALL TO MEMORY
He now is left with nothing for himself.

14

On his retreat from Ararat,
midway along the anxious path
that veered for years but led him back
to Chelm, a pensive ararite
had bought a plate from Rhodes that caught—
with penetrating tenderness—
two images that left him less
disconsolate. He found it at
the sprawling *souk* of Smyrna,
in the stall of the melanous merchant,
in the month of al-Muhárram.

He meant the plate to serve as gift
for all the pindarites of Chelm
(who stayed within the walls and shunned
far heights and said the way to seek
the past was surely underneath
and not among evasive peaks);
and on this plate, where one might see
two sisters, pictured frontally,§
their shoulders draped in bayaderes
as graceful as the birds of air,
the ararite inscribed with care:

This russet plate from Rhodes has two gazelles:
their grey eyes pair these decasyllables.

----

§*Some say the ararite*
 had seen no figuration:
 it was the sisters he had seen
 beneath the light of Smyrna quays—
 within the flesh, foreshadowing
 the perfect woman.

15

And when he hears Ravel's
   groundswell,
   "*A–sie!*
     A––sie!
       A–––sie!"
   he does not flee
   to Smyrna.

Instead,
   by lantern light and when
   that lantern light is spent,
   he plans

   portulans

   for shores no man of Chelm had met
   (except by way of sad shipwrecks)

   and sets his patient pen to etch
   arabesques:

   inlets
   and coves
   and sinuous
   sandbars
   and haunting harbors
   and hanging crags
   and pliant stone
   and breasts of nymphs
   who want their warm
   delirium
   beneath the sun

along the shoals
or tender sands—
where waves may find abandon—
or cool transfiguration
within more pensive shelters,
beside the nenuphars
on unobtrusive
waters.

With eyes intent
while spine is bent,
he does not lift
his lens or stay
his unrelenting
pen—neglect
even the least
or last of bays,
the final reef,
the farthest reach
of anthozoan coral

until

the waves
of Asia
of Ravel

settle.

16

The cranes,
the herons
never stay
beyond the
second day
of Heshvan.

And then—
some say—
they make
their way
to Smyrna.

THE THIRD FINDING NOW IS FOUND

CESURASONG THREE

for the interval between
the Third and Fourth Findings

To be sure,
non sequitur.

And yet—to veer
is also answer.

THE FOURTH FINDING
of maxioms/maxims/axioms

וכוא הלך להתבודד צין הריס

1

By now he totters to be sure,
but Zeno's tortoise crawls—secure—
in Chelm;

not one man here would dream
of overtaking him.§

2

The tortoise that was dropped on Aeschylus
is absolutely not to be confused
with the intrepid tortoise Zeno used:

the first is served in bits in flat fish-soups;
the second studied sapid recipes
from Syracuse to Chelm—in cordon bleus

where secret sprig and spice were sauced—and fused
infinitesimally-diced-hare stews,
dismaying dish no savant could refuse,§§

then took a trenchant look at Machiavelli's
fine arts. His course is done and now he sees
how soft are strongmen's parts. He stews Achilles.

---

§*And he was never alien:*
for—after all—the pindarites
would welcome one from Elea
who, drawn by their dismaying psalms,
had entered into maxioms
(as many sentences have done)
by way of the Gate of Phantom.

§§*Some read* ragouts *for* stews *and some refuse*
refuse; *instead they choose to read* refute,
redargue—*more successive substitutes—*
while fingering their paraphrastic lutes
or tallying the lint on black surtouts.

3

Achilles never would have sulked in Chelm,
for we have never had an Agamemnon.

4

But—then again—he might have missed
the burnished arms of Myrmidons,
Patroclus in his clanging bronze—
a tribe without a tent in our tradition,
the elders seemed to frown upon that camp—

yet some persistent Winckelmann
of Chelm—we have had more than one—
could have obtained permission
for him to bring them with him
quietly—and *ohne* fuss—
for long maneuvers in the dusk,

his Myrmidons,
his Patroclus.

5

Eleven lucid scrutinists
insist the tortoise lives in *ignes*

fatui and phantom mists,
in catabatic labyrinths

so fictive he must be dismissed:
Achilles never trembled with

despair—with that antagonist.§

6

And yet the twelfth is adamant:
he has condemned as sham and cant
attempts to pierce the "phantom mists"
derisively—to fault or scant
the force that lives in labyrinths.
He chants—instead—the Phantom Chant:

The phantom feeds on stillness.
The phantom feeds on fracas.

The phantom feeds on amphibrachs,
on Agri Dagis, Ararats,

on waves and woodways and the veer
of sinuous non sequiturs,

elusive glides and fricatives
and turbid liquids; and he lives

on any will that will not rest
in Pumbeditha or the Besht,

---

§*And others added here: nor did the hare,
unless he still was lame from earlier
encounters—when he had to race Despair
and leaped across that monster, landing nowhere
or—some say—in the fountain in our square.*

[71]

or in the lens from Amsterdam
or Underwood of Mandelstam,

but wanders all of them—or none—
on phantom paralimnions.

Beneath the light of lakeside quays
and lantern light, the phantom feeds

on far more phemes that never near
unless the phantom stands to hear,

on *Vast and Versal Lexicons*
and on hallucinariums,

on lizards' flight, on karaites,
on palimpsests, on pindarites'

paeans, Schliemanns, citrons,
and on the perfect woman;

but neither stillness, fracas, all
of Chelm—inhabitants and walls—

can fill his duodenum:
the phantom is a cavern.

The phantom is a mountain;
the span of his jejunum

is more than any pararhyme
can fathom with its plummet line;

Goliath is a gonium
against the girth of phantom; Samson—

tresses at the full—is less
than just one hair upon his chest;

and on his lectern—where no tent
of myrmidon would more than speck—

sanhedrins of Saadya Gaons
grumble but must grovel when

he burnishes and brandishes
his shafts of exegesis:

the phantom casts a javelin
beyond the reach of reason

and then a second javelin
beyond the force of fiction,

and—last—without a let,
one single breath and flex—

he casts a eucalyptus
beyond the force of force.

The phantom is a forest.
The phantom is an isthmus.

He has dismaying sinews,
the power and the ruse:

the boulders he can lift,
behemoth cannot shift;

the mazes he can track,
Mercator did not map;

The dances he can dance
leave fanfaronade wan,

and rodomontade pants
before the phantom's done

with sarabands of resonance
and farandoles of difference,

and then—upon the other hand—
with sarandole and faraband.

The phantom is a fountain.
The phantom has a yataghan.

He leaps upon leviathan;
no whirlwind can defeat him.

He rides astonished axioms;
no lemma can unseat him.

When he would camp in caves of doubt
no faith can ever thrust him out.

When he would vagabond with trust,
no doubt can tempt, insidious.

When he is bent on paradox,
the straightest arrow ends in knot;

and yet no text can twist him back,
he cracks the hardest hapax.

The phantom's galimatias
can overwhelm sagacious.

The phantom finds a limit.
The phantom passes it.

The phantom is a desert.
The phantom's thirst is endless.

He is more swift, more agonist
than any pensive tortoise.

7

Promiscuous savants—
who want to answer every want
and dance with any wanton gloss—
when lantern light is low enough,
vagabond with this
embracing exegesis:

The tortoise agonistes and—as well—
the shell that held the helpless animal
that fell as in a fatal tarantella
(dismaying dance they often dance in Gela,
with tortoises and Greeks and evil eagles)
upon the burnished crown of Aeschylus—

are not to be confused
with any tortoise crawling toward Peru
that offered haunting clues
to Darwin when he danced the Galapagos.

8

Still others cried that Captain Cook
   first spied these tacit tortoises;
   but if he looked, he did not see
(or if he saw, he overlooked)
   their logogriphs, for they were too
   elusive for the use of Cook
(not that his glass was that obtuse—
   the savant in him knew the truth
   was tottering before his lens;
and yet, although he watched it wend,
   he could not comprehend its end,
   the whence and where and why it went
the way of swaying tortoises);
   instead of Cook a man of Kent
   (since Chelm was very slow to send
its pensive missions overseas)
   was needed to decipher these,
   to meet the meanings that they meant.
And so they held their cryptic shells
   another sixty years; and while
   they overlooked the blue-grey swell
that foamed and fell toward far Peru,
   within their brooding latitude
   they dreamt upon their rendezvous

with Darwin.

9

The dance that Darwin danced:
the arabesque of evidence,
where man and datum stretch—
to point of consummation.

10

Upon the cold Carpathians
the dance the Besht had danced was one
for man and will in unison.

11

Why did the Besht not dance on Ararat?
Perhaps he did not want to dance on past.

12

No crane, no heron flies
to Ararat or Agri Dagi:
those mountains are too dry.

THE FOURTH FINDING NOW IS FOUND

CESURASONG FOUR

for the interval between
the Fourth and Fifth Findings

I

To tell a tale
entails a line—

of ebb and rise,
climb and decline,

or wane and swell,
and wax and fall—

but sons of Chelm
are nursed on why's

and knot the wax
and foul the fall

and twist the guise
and then forget

why they had ever
told at all—

and some say they
can hardly tell.

II
How hazardous—
when tellers try

to thread an act
through the eye

of syntax; yet

if sense is thin
or eye is gross,

that passage is
less arduous.

THE FIFTH FINDING
of maxioms/axioms/maxims

איכה יסבה 773

1

Emancipation drummed.

(At scumbled dawn, dismaying forms
gathered at the gates of Chelm.)

And some would dream Jerusalem
where time to be revealed was come:

The wailing walls where all can weep.

The All beyond the parts of speech.

The lawns where labyrinths can reach
the light in vast and versal dance.

A Jacobin
Jerusalem,

where even truth was citizen
and every month—either/or
Germinal/Floréal,

a lucid land, Humanistan,
more spacious than
Elysium

or Albion
or Athens.

But some now walk the narrow one:

They say revehent time is less
than time to be revealed—and yet
to live is not constriction.

2

He is alive:
let him live.

3

Guilt is the shell and I am in it.

So said the poet from Milan,
a frequent visitor to Chelm.

That likeness lets him conjure exit.

But how not stay within it,
sin it,
when the shell is infinite?

4

But others held
that what he held

was right:
the shell

is finite, that
it can be cracked.

5

Still others held
we do not dwell
within or past
but at the shell,

just as—some add—

we do not wait
within or past
the patient walls
of Chelm but at

the patient gates.

6

The shell
is wall.

The shell
is shore.

The shell
is far

from pure.

7

Speech is touch—

not smooth, rough, just
hardness, softness, but

at point of utterance,
already wound, caress:

sang Levinas.

8

Along the plain of Exile
beneath the patient foothills,

whenever men of Chelm have told
of time that is to be revealed—

the is may equal may or shall;
for Exile had one patient wall

to shield the possible as well
as one against the possible.

It was the last that fell.

9

Do not defend the ways of men
to God and not the ways of God
to men for each of them has turned
aside and each has found it hard
to listen when the other was
the one who was in question and
for each the one atonement is:
              begin again.

10

A son of Chelm had written these
wallwords on entering an oven
and whispered them again when he
had let me dream of him within
my room above the Isar when
the waters crossing Munich seemed
to murmur, asking if one can
begin again and answering
within a voice they took from him:
              Begin, begin.

11

"And what is that Galician Jew
doing here?" *Nec spe nec metu,*

Frantisek
Kriegel, Jew and pseudo-Czech,

had heard
the syllables that fell—
like excrement of animals—

above a square that could have held
a hundred squares of Chelm but not

one fountain.

12

He is alive,
but let him live.

13

O bitter Heshvan,
most autumnal
month, the orphan

month deprived
of feasts,

at last I reach
your autumn:
we can meet

to fill
your vacant vigils,

beside
a total table

to tell
the chronicles

of what—
because it lived—
is lost

and, in the circle
of recall,

inscribe the rhombus
of an all:

autumnal—yet
intact.

14

Maxioms
malign sixteens
blessings
blind ingatherings
branchings
trees
clarities
stammerings
exegeses
auguries
seeds

stupidities
rememberings
praisings
dreams
forgettings
rantings
screams
phlegm
a volume
Chelm
had bound
adorned
meticulous
until
it found
the leaves
were loose
and fell
as blood
on ground
grown unfamiliar

15

The will that would traverse—
as would the crane—the earth

deserts.

THE FIFTH FINDING NOW IS FOUND

CESURASONG FIVE

*for the interval between
the Fifth and Sixth Findings*

seed : thread : drum

: :

point : line : volume

THE SIXTH FINDING
the Men of Chelm Have Seen the Perfect Woman

שמי

שמולה

לקנות אותה

ע״י עמל והשתדלות

היא רחוקה יותר מפנינים

ממקומס במעלות ים רחוקים

ולריך לעצור ימים רחוקים

ולרדת למעמקי

מצולות

What plight or premonition
had led the perfect woman
to enter Chelm? What thought
had interrupted thought?
Some said she overheard
the phantom chant, and some,
the rasp of the hoarse savant.
And others add: The shadows
that shelter nesting birds
along the silent lakes,
the silent ponds, the marshes,
the estuaries—all
the waters of the night
that lie upon the earth
beside the birds of air—
had seen her bayadere
and scattered when she crossed
the Gate of the Event.

Two/ THE PERFECT WOMAN READS
A PAGE OF KANT

The perfect woman reads a page of Kant.
She thinks upon the mauve invariants
of later August and the pregnant branch
of slender gestruemia, on the *Selbst-*
erkenntniss of this island in the lake,
upon the arbor and the silent wakes
of silent boats, of all that need not take
hellways to find their godliness but glide
or rest or hover on the silent waters
and do not shudder at the fate of fire

or tremble at the final sun that fills
the steep arena of these patient foothills
until the revery, the reverence
are cracked, the sun become a second Vulcan,
herself a Venus for the Lord of Flame,
the pensive arsonist who can proclaim
the fire that enters every secret seam
of stone or leaf or flesh, a deity
beneath whose blows the hide of things is torn
and all that is at last is read as one

or ashes. She reflects, as on an urn,
upon *flammantia moenia mundi*, fallen
walls of the world, the burning boundaries
that held the Alps, the straining galaxies,
and all the wind-whipped dead: the sentry house
is cinders; border guardians, sages, friends
are gone; her journey need not be clandestine.
Alone, the perfect woman steps across
the ford of air, taking from Vulcan not
his bolts and brands of fire, but his art

and metals. And she flails the air until
her arms become her oars, the silent waters
retreat before the hammers of her want,
and flight of meaning finds her clutching at
regret, the final flower found by Kant.

Three/ SINGSONGS FOR THE
PERFECT WOMAN

sung

by

eleven

men

of

Chelm

at

times

in

unison

and

some-

times

one

by

one

Why should she read Spinoza in her tent?

2/

Before the cadence of her neck
Parmigianino would have kept
astonished silence.

3/ *A Thing Is a Monotonous Event*

She knows that Chelm has never known a Lent.

4/

The lash of Virgo's sun is less
than her shoulders.

She thinks on good men in their thingliness.

6/

Flowering
as if possessed
by waves
of mauve
exuberance,
the gestruemia
may mime
but not surpass
her dress.

7| *She Thinks of Good Men in Their*
   Thingliness

She asks if true volcanoes can be spent.

8/ *The Ayre of the Rhomboid Fountain*

The perfect woman would observe
the waters of the fountain curve.

Yet even as she finds their fall
and rise, she reads no parable.

The azure of her eyes resists
the rites of the analogist.

She sees the waters. That is all.
The azure rise. The azure fall.

The fate of that particular.

9/ *The Lied of the Distant Sands*

I

And shall we ever walk the walls
of Saint-Malo together;

or, even as the tides advance
with anabatic calligraphs,

decide instead to turn our backs
and, having taken counterpaths,

to meet where semicircles reach,
while each repeats the variants

that he or she has harvested,
refused, recast, or left intact

[106]

along divided ways we chose
whenever we would walk—

and gloss the sands below—
the walls of Saint-Malo?

II
Or shall we never walk the walls
of Saint-Malo at all

and let the ramparts scan the sands
or overlook the breakers,

and stay within the stones of Chelm
and gaze at them
and at each other

and only leave to sail along
the western paralimnion

or else—when I walk on alone,
and north, into the forest,

beyond the edge of autumn—
to gather gynoecia

for you—to let the anthers
rest gently on your fingers—

to find and free
the fragrance

of eucalyptus
in the winter.

Long since, in solemn visits—
by lantern light and then
beneath the light of Deneb—
it shared elusive logogriphs
and hypograms with him;

yet he had read some reticence,
some thing withheld in all its gifts,
a letter lost, omitted,
a tremor of mistrust, as if
a slightest flaw in fellowship

(born of his own impatience
for total invitation?);
but now—at last—Delirium,
beneath the moon of Heshvan,
had murmured: "*Vade mecum.*"

Pell mell, he left the walls of Chelm
and went the way of tacit trees—
the north, the silence, the nuance
of black and taupe and granite trunks—
to meet that final summons

(he followed a discolored scroll
that mapped the forest in a scrawl
as labyrinthine as a soul
that wanders endless texts
that it may be made whole);

but even as he travelled on
across the metamorphic leaves
that still lay loose on autumn ground
before the snow had packed them down,
he fell upon the perfect woman.

And when he saw her bayadere,
more brilliant than the birds of air,
in green and gold and azure,
the shadows that awaited him
seemed dregs of death and error;

and when he heard her voice that used
the parts of speech as plants have used
the water and the air,
converting them—dull elements
and colorless—to living fare,

he veered about and south with her—
and let distraught Delirium
await some other son of Chelm
to share oblique soliloquies
along woodways and cryptic leagues.

11/ *The Song of Song*

We are your subtlest instruments:

no music branches to your breasts
that does not sound in us,

no music dies away from you
that in us lives not,

and even in your absence
your cadence journeys, just

as—once—the northwind touched,
while the exhausted psalmist slept,

upon the lyre in his tent
until it had awakened him;

and even when he was away
that wind called David back—some say—

and those who so assert
are those who know the force

that strings can summon when
they are taut—

the force of us.

Four/ THE PERFECT WOMAN SEES SOME MEN OF CHELM

Ah! non credea

mirarti

1/ *The Song of Sorts*

I

Sages, Savants, Elders, Rabbis,
Fathers, Forebears, Omnivores,
Epigraphers and Picadors,
Emenders, Mendicants, Embalmers,
Massoretes and Exegetes,
the None, the Melanous, the Wan,
the Pure, the Sure, the Sepulchers,

and Staggards, Prickets, Brockets, Fawns,
and Maggots, Pismires, Mastodons,
the Genesists, the Exodists,
the Nebulists, the Unconvinced,
the Nettles, Tares, the Terebinths,
the Stratocumuli, the Wisps,
the Digits, Cubists, Septuagints,

the Fathoms and the Fathomless,
the Vines, the Vats, the Trellises,
the Awed, the Flawed, the Tortoises,
the Quandarists and Quamoclits,
Amphibolists and Tamarisks,
the Seeds, the Bees, the Wicks, the Wax,
the Honeycombs, the Nectarless,

and Fireflies and *Flammenwerfers*,
Polyhistors, Rhetors, Wreckers,
Mirrors, Makers, Scavengers,
the Reverend, the Renegade,
the Herons, Cranes, the Unallayed,
Innocuists and Evanescents,
Palimpsests and Pomegranates,

the Arks, the Floods, the Ararats,
the Fatuists, the Unabashed,
the Doves, the Vulturine, the Gnats,
the Vines, the Trellises, the Vats,
the Carrefours, the Culs-de-sac,
the Underwood, the Lush, the Rank,
the Roots, the Rot, the Paraphrasts,

and Sciolists and Scoriasts
and Boulders, Brambles, Yarrow, Grass,
the Guides, the Guises, the Aghast:
how difficult to carve or limn
the sure distinctions that divide,
that—once the lake is crossed or dusk
dismantles every plain—will last.

    II
The only certainty: that Scribes
(more bilious men than those above)
are not content to be alive

except when sabbath falls or love
descends or ends—or names that lie
in labyrinths awake and writhe

and slough their skins and ask for light
or—quiet, penitent—consent
to leave the furrowed text, to die.

2/ *The Song of Eye*

The visible incites the eye
but the unseen invites his mind.

I

And if the new man, in forgetfulness
of his conversion, were to watch the russet
of eucalyptus branches that—a lustrum
and more—had lived upon his mantle; if
unmindful of his metamorphic gifts,
his vision knelt along the red prayer-rug,
and he found ancient measure of himself,
a measure made of openness and stealth,

within the walls he knew, before the dust
of patient and impatient books he had read,
the same green ink, two letters from the dead
poet, the pack that bears in white and blue
and black the adjective for *veritas*,
that filters toxins to a residue
which, although fatal, is innocuous:
would new or old be truer or be true?

II

Or if he cast aside the castanets
of "lustrum," "russet," "dust" as vulgar clacks
of shells that shook when time struck hard against
the hide of emptiness with non-events,
the mendicant flamenco of his mind,
the fracas and fiasco of a line,
the habit of the uninhabited,
bedraggled semblances of ritual,

and saw instead that there was neither rhyme
nor pararhyme that chimed within his acts,
that all he mimed was unrepeating, un-
repentant, nothing added now could sum
with what had been subtracted, every room
or noon as random as hullabaloo,
however long his life revised, he'd still
not find the full and final anagram:

would hopelessness become his last content?

4/ *A Lantern Song*

He has forgotten azure.
He lives beneath a lantern.
More pallid. More sure.

The razor worn to gravel, to be scrapped.
   The glass that can't remember to reflect,
     fogged by the steam of the untaken bath,

or cracked.
   The hand is poised, but cannot act
     or react.

Hair of the head, hair of the body,
   semen, nails: the sole events.
     All else relents

into the elaborate
   adagio of aimlessness.
     Right hand then left drum on a sink.

The eyes are thirsty, drink
   their own dismay.
     Blinking, bearded, he

strides out, in four-four time,
   to single combat with the sun,
     declaiming to another day

along the disconcerted quays
   at dawn, above the pliant reeds
     that tremble even as he roars

or chants or rasps or soughs or murmurs.

6/ Second Chant of the Hoarse Savant

And even as she heard him sing:

"*At one in our illusion*
what is the difference between
that Frenchman from Calvados,
Jude Stefan, who wrote
in 'Inexistence' quote,

'*Alike in our illusion*
what is the difference
between that Chinese poet
of the eighteenth century
by their reckoning

Lu Tan Tong the naive one
who spoke once telling of
the vanishings of form
because the waters flow away
one morning the rose was

undone each day must fade
and that old man is gone
beneath the tree that lives on—
and me this anonymous one
of clouds and sleeplessness?

difference of tone he on
the lake me on the bed
perceived by none,' unquote Stefan—
and me a labyrinthine one
transcribing in another tongue

along the sleepless quays that line
another lake—the lake of Chelm—
watched over by a distant pair
whose words—like nesting nightbirds
so loud within their rest—

appear at once within my ear
and theirs—three men
watched over by the absent ones
who built the gates that carry all
away from Chelm and back again?"—

she did not interrupt. She thought.

7/ *First Song of Scavenging*

Abundant or autumnal branches:
both have served his uses.

8/ *Second Song of Scavenging*

It's not that he forgets. But the endured
is more than can be rendered.

How they crack:
the word and the appeasing act.

But even as they shatter,
he gathers fragmentary matter.

9/ *The Song of Offspring*

And as you wait for the enormous Sadness
to take his place upon that high-backed chair,

his three great heads, three jaws that would dismember
the future, present, past, as you prepare

cheeses and demijohns to dam his hunger,
distracting scrolls—your most tenacious labor—

to keep his eyes from you, remember:
that monster is the son that we have fathered,

his form was born out of our love, our anger.

10/ Cavesong

Some men of Chelm have watched their need retreat
into a grotto hard as diamond;
and there, immobile, glittering, it waits
until they see that cavern is their fate
and, blinded by relentless facets, weep.

Yet when the lights of autumn sift
the faces we should mourn or miss
were we to visit lakeside quays
and find nuance of wave and mist
but not the voice that answered us,
then she remembers one—and with
insistent tenderness—who kept
a flock of scumbled images:
he herded correspondences
for all that breathes or is inert
within a pen that mimed the egg
where Adam, being wrought, had raged—
a shell of names that shook and split
wherever likeness did not fit
the rites of the analogist;
no sooner was he unassuaged
than he assembled his disheveled
semblances and sheared their edges,
that he might shepherd them again
through stretto passages that ran—
as in a frugal fret—to one
                hallucinarium.

And she had shared his years and fears
and gathered up his fallen shears
and slowly, softly made it plain—
as one who chants the low refrain
a child demands to still its pain—

that edges, even as they cut,
are but the way the earth would thrust
itself on oval consciousness;
and she has overlooked the trials,
the rotting wood, the rusted nails,
dismaying planes, and twisted awls
of carpenters of total tables;
and never damned, disdained, disprized—
and always nourished with her eyes—
          dismantled scribes.

And when the quaeres that perplex
the pandects of the Oral Law
obsessed a fervent elder, who
would only leave his lectern for
a lectern down the corridor,
she reconciled his writhing texts,
she set to rest his quodlibets;
no less, the light, the love she shed
upon a pindarite, distressed
along a restless, rhomboid path
among benighted taupe and black;
and when he met the labyrinths
of meter for his mazing hymns
and stumbled on a cryptic foot
and cried his hurt until dayspring,
she did not turn to silence him
but shared her lucid disciplines;

and often—when a single verse
of their one source had left them worse
than when they'd heard the verse before—
with silence, in her slender arms,
she held the only healing for
        ecclesiastesists.

How much a pensive woman can—
her epithet is valiant,
the sages say, her worth is past
the worth of pearls—but she is wan
within the alleyways of Chelm,
where dwell revehent time as well
as undismayed delirium,
that claims to be the final flame
of reason, when it cannot help
but soar, and sears, consumes itself,
and gutters into nameless wax
or burns away to shapeless ash,
the cinders of non sequitur
beneath the inaccessible azure:
she needs a hearth to keep her warm
but not a charnel house; she wants
a forest free of bedlam trees,

an arbor free of bedlam plants,
a vase in which a stem can stand
alone—and still be understood—
without the mauve extravagance
with which a scribe in heat has danced
          the gestruemia—

not that she would malign his lines
or scant the savage labor pains
he takes with first and second paeons;
for she has seen him dance the sands
of Saint-Malo when tides advanced,
with calligraphs, against his balance
(his semes mean well—just that his mind
will often heave in waves of wine—
witness the song he sang awry
on Venus, Kant, and burning walls
and arson, anything at all
so long as his long surf might swell
at each successive interval),
and she acknowledges that he
has always been meticulous
whenever he has singsung on
          the eucalyptus.

Six/ THE CANTILENA OF THE CRANE

Beneath the eucalyptus branches
one crane advances. On a path
that overlaps another path—

as ask and answer intersect
in furrowed texts or fugal fret
of stretto passages—one crane

advances. On its candid back,
in black surtout, a hoarse savant—
stringent—chants of Ararat

and of the intricate soutache
upon the perfect woman's dress.

THE SIXTH FINDING NOW IS FOUND

AFTERSONGS
for the first Six Findings

AFTERSONG 1 | *Title page*

The name of Chelm has never lurked
or wandered in the wanton smoke

of Smyrna's dens with dark *chibouque*
or *chaff* or *charlatan* or *churl*.

To chant of *Chelm* is to recall
an ancient spring, a deeper well,

the tenderest of gutturals:
the *ch* that sings in *nachtigall*.

AFTERSONG 2 | *Epigraph*

Midway on his evasive path
    the journeyman from Ararat
    had overhead Spinoza's words;
but others—ill at ease with rough
    paraphrase—have long preferred:
    Se in somnis non habere potestatem cogitandi

quod vellet, et quod non vellet scribere;
    nec, cum somniat se velle scribere,
    potestatem habet non somniandi
se velle scribere. And more
    assiduous interpreters—
    aware of all the veering ear

can gather when dispirited—
    are sure he also heard a Berber
    chant of faith and loss and fear:
Siwelt aɣ d nebɣ' a-n-nas
    lɣerba atas
    iɣab yisem iw ur yehdir—

though some allow he may have found
   the cadence of the *Isefra*
  of flawless Si Mohand-ou-Mhand
within a version—far more raw—
   that Mouloud Mammeri had murmured:
  Rappelez-moi je veux revenir

Trop longue a été mon absence
  Mon nom perdu s'est oublié.
  Words that wait along woodway.

AFTERSONG 3 | *Gatesong 1*

The *Vast and Versal Lexicon*—
which, when it would, can still inform—
notes: *Ges-tru-é-mi-a* was once
the *la-ger-stroe-mi-a*, for one
Herr Magnus Lagerstroem, a Swede
(to be exact, Linnaeus had
made him the patron of its seeds).

Its *la* was then mistaken for
an Agrigentine article;
deprived of that, it found an *r*
was lost when seven hoarse savants
insisted that the buccal dance
cannot withstand four consonants
that cluster in inelegance.

And from *ges-troe-mi-a* the reach
to *ges-tru-é-mi-a* was brief:
one diphthong found itself prolonged,
two vowels were spawned where there was one,
the former altered—and the tree
of Chelm was ready for the quays.

Some say the lean eleven trees
that lined the disconcerted quays

were planted by eleven tribes
that, guided by eleven scribes,

arrived by way of plain or lake
or stranger ways that overtake

the walker when he least expects
a lucid path through tattered texts:

analogists and ararites
and agonists and pindarites

and legalists and spinozists
and kabalists and tortoisists

and brusque ecclesiastesists§
and metamorphosists, to which

the hoarse savant would add a sect
that fed on likelihood and thus

made do with meagerness—the wise.

---

§*They had been called kohelethites*
until a long addendum in
the Vast and Versal Lexicon
on "More Phemes Chelm Alone Has Known"
left them ecclesiastesists—

and here the hoarse savant would warn:
The restless sect that wants to dance
the dance of onomasticon
may stumble out of seemliness
unless it keeps its sibilants

in hand.

AFTERSONG 5 | *Gatesong 2*

Six scholiasts who never slept
until their lens—incensed—had tracked
the *Countermaxioms*' palimpsest,

with tattered evidence at hand—
a semi-uncial hand—contend:
The codex came as contraband,

brought by a beardless discontent
(who had deserted Chelm for wealth
and carried off six scrolls by stealth)

to Smyrna—where disheveled eyes,
that gybe and writhe with wanton lies,
fed on its *ignes fatui*—

in the stall of the melanous merchant.

AFTERSONG 6 | *Gatesong 3*

The *Vast and Versal Lexicon*'s
eleven enchiridions—
through sage miscegenation—spawned

an unassuming organon,
where parts of speech from every tongue
the men of Chelm have maundered, moaned,

berated, blathered, clishmaclavered,
chanted, ranted, rasped, and soughed—
can now consort, caress, then rest

in order alphabetical—
discreet and cordial carnival—
without a word that wakes disheveled;

and since the path Uighurian
or Ugaritic runs is one
Kashubish, Slovintzish, Yakoot,

and Wishram, Wasco, Chuvash, Ute
have shunned, the *Versal Lexicon*
beguiles with boustrophedon—but

arrays each word from its far end
to ease the pains of journeymen
intent on *rima franta, rime*

couée, croisée, batelée, melée,
brisée, and pararhymes and chimes
that haunt the lines of leonines.

Yet scribes who savor consonants—
averring vowels are merely breath
and pneuma cannot vie with flesh

(a tenet Smyrna's dens abet)—
have often tended to neglect
each entry bent on assonance,

for though it may sit well with ours,
it seldom seems to fit their *ars.*

AFTERSONG 7 / *First Finding • Maxiom 3*

I

The sedentaries
seldom left

the total table
but they sat

away from its
evasive edge.

I I

And six insist
that those who sit

away from an
evasive edge

are better called
analogists.

AFTERSONG 8 | *First Finding · Maxiom 13*

Against a metamorphosist
whose shadow intersected his,

the hoarse savant would rage and sough:
"But '*les nuages ont des dessins*

aussi fermés que ceux des hommes' "—
and having soughed, he staggered on

to watch an altostratus stray
across a stratocumulus

until it had recovered just
the norm, the form alloted it—

despite the metamorphosists.

Ten say Spinoza's lens
saw Chelm from Amsterdam,

and nine say Amsterdam
from Chelm; and eight contend

his lens took One too far,
and seven, far too near;

six murmur, it was polished,
and five, by no means clear;

four chant, it saw too much,
three rant, not quite enough,§

for where it saw our bondage,
it overlooked our rage;

and two have long insisted
that, with that Sephardi's lens,

whatever was the angle
of light in incidence,

one surely saw as well
as through the glass of angels;

and one says, not at all,
for it was monocle.

---

§*And some say, just enough—
and more than the* pandoche
*of Leibniz (as it strikes the eye
in his* Notitia opticae
        promotae).

The hoarse savant once thought upon
one leg—as heron, crane have done
on pensive paralimnions.

He did not stand on speech alone,
He did not stand on speechlessness.
He did not stand upon a text.

He simply stood upon one leg.
Yet—even as he watched a sun
almost as wan as Heshvan's sun

abandon island, lake, and hill
to grey nuance of wave and mist
without one voice that answered his—

he did not stand upon it long
before he had contemned the rest
of tutelary birds upon

that listless paralimnion.

AFTERSONG 11 | *Second Finding • Maxiom 11*

That karaite was distant kin—
six sing—of Zerach bar Nathan,
contentious Lithuanian,

whose quaeres Joseph Salomon
Del Médigo had answered in
Een Rabbinsch Mathematisch Boeck—

on which Spinoza's lens—beneath
the lucid lantern light that reached
his eucalyptus lectern—looked.

AFTERSONG 12 / *Second Finding · Maxiom 11*

Two syncretistic connoisseurs
of unashamed non sequiturs
have long contended they are sure:

The karaitic maxiom
must be the chant Apollinaire
had had in mind when he averred,

*"Il y a un poème à faire
sur l'oiseau qui n'a qu'une aile."*

AFTERSONG 13 / *Second Finding · Maxiom 12*

Six say *the the* was later sung
by one—his beard well-dressed—who thrummed
of Haddam, Adam, Farmington.

How far was Farmington from Chelm?
As far as gestruemia
and eucalyptus are from elm.

AFTERSONG 14 / *Third Finding · Maxiom 4*

The pindarites remembered that—
while cold and sad in Petrograd,
where he had sung in manuscript
before an Underwood was his—
young Mandelstam had chanted this:

*In diaphanous Petropolis we die,
where she who rules as queen is Proserpine.*

*With every breath we drink the fatal air,
a year of death for us in every hour.*

Goddess of the sea, awesome Athena,
lay down your heavy helmet made of stone.

In diaphanous Petropolis we die—
here you are not the queen, but Proserpine.

AFTERSONG 15 | *Third Finding · Maxiom 4*

Six say the *Echte Pinakothek*
of Chelm was without walls except
the walls of Chelm itself;§

and three consider even these
but unenlightened boundaries—

the true museum is the mind,
though it is often hard to find

the curator.§§

AFTERSONG 16 | *Third Finding · Maxiom 8*

Beneath their pallid lanterns,
within the mists of Heshvan,
the pindarites would dream
of golden Agrigentum
because of Pythian Twelve,
an ode that never left
their eucalyptus shelves;

---

§*A Frenchman later*
  introduced this practice elsewhere.

§§*A Frenchman—earlier—*
  was certain he or—rather—
  his cogito *was curator.*

just as a son of Sète
in black surtout and vest,
when he was most perplexed,
abandoned dochmiacs
but never could forget
the force of Pythian Three
in chanting of a seaside cemetery.

AFTERSONG 17 | *Third Finding • Maxiom 10*

The *Deutung* they assigned to *Traum*
was never ominous in Chelm
until Vienna whelmed.

AFTERSONG 18 | *Third Finding • Maxiom 13*

Not that the pindarite would scant
the lash of the revehent past;
and six—aghast—have heard him chant
twice over, in a tongue more rude
than any Pindar ever used:

Memini etiam quae nolo,
oblivisci non possum quae volo—
though three aver he murmured: *I*
recall what I would not recall
and what I would forget, I can't.

AFTERSONG 19 | *Third Finding • Maxiom 15*

Were these the shores where Monsieur Teste,
a sedentary son of Sète,
had shed his black surtout, his vest,
and, with his stylus set, had wantoned:
sur le sable tendre ou s'abandonne
                    l'onde?

The hoarse savant was heard to rasp:
The phantom danced the buccal dance

with
spirants
glottals
sibilants
occlusives
labials
laterals
fricative trills
fricative laterals
laminals
nasals
dentals
palatals
palatal-alveolars
lamino-alveolars
lamino-dentals

and

alveolars
apicals
apico-alveolars
ejectives
ingressives
implosives
flaps
stops
clicks
as
well
as
simple
glides
and
liquids.
The phantom mouth was never one
to savor unrefined distinctions.

The
Chelm
Sanhedrin
always
met
on
every
even
day
except
when
even
fell
on
odd
because
of
over
whelming
rest
lessness

That eucalyptus—was it *alba*?
Pauciflora?   *Maculata*?
Ficifólia?   *Deglupta*?

Coriácea?   *Cordupta*?
Resinífera?   Or just
(as breathless ararites assert—

whenever scudding in subfusc
of forests where the rush of dusk
along woodways outraces trust)

a eucalyptus?

The poet from Milan—
Giovanni Giudici—
mislaid an Olivetti
within the walls of Chelm.

When found—six say—it stood
beside the Underwood
that Osip Mandelstam
had used in nineteen-twenty-

four-and-five. And many
have found a force that few
can ever call upon,
the force of Mandelstam,

in the poet from Milan.

AFTERSONG 24
   Sixth Finding • The Ayre of Apparition

What plight is not a plight of Chelm?
Chelm is the portulan for plights.

AFTERSONG 25
   Sixth Finding • The Lied of the Distant Sands

How far was Saint-Malo from Chelm?
How distant, Agrigentum?

No farther than the phantom casts—
when snow is at the Gate of Text

and even lantern light is spent—
the javelin of longing.

AFTERSONG 26 / *Sixth Finding · The Lied of Yet*

I

And was the intricate soutache
that hemmed the perfect woman's dress
worn on the form of Greta Lentz?

Or did that pensive woman bear
another name when she appeared
before the hoarse savant's flecked beard:

Mme. Ébauche? Mme. Debauch?
Frau Aziman? Or Frau Conortz?
And did a pindarite distort

when—suddenly—he chanted: She
(when met in revery or dream,
within the walls or on dim quays,

bypaths, or in parentheses
that intersect the violence
of all that is with peace that seems)

was called Signora Enthymeme?

II

Or is the distant voice that pleads
in unison with ancient need
(despite the metamorphosists'

persistent murmur: To define
defiles the dress, the nakedness,
the black surtout, the gold soutache,

the gaze of eye, the gaze of flesh,
the patient passacaglia and
the calculating saraband,

[143]

the turbulence, the calm caress,
the thraws and throes, the helplessness
of man and woman, breast on breast)

when—from the undiminished shadows
past the lantern's pallid halo—
quietly, it says: I know

her name was surely Gaia Canso.

THE AFTERSONGS NOW ARE FOUND

SCORIAE

from *The Vast & Versal Lexicon*

בדקדוק גדול ובחקירה רבה

> For the diction
> of this treatise has not been chosen at
> haphazard, but with great exactness and
> exceeding precision, and with care to a-
> void failing to explain any obscure point.
> And nothing has been mentioned out of its
> place, save with a view to explaining some
> matter in its proper place.

ABELARD—Before and between his condemnations at Soissons (1121) and Sens (1140), Abelard was preoccupied with the Trinity (in his *Tractatus de Unitate et Trinitate Divina*—discovered and edited by Stölzle in 1891—and its recasting in his *Theologia Christiana*; and in his *Sic et Non*). But sciolists note that the Trinity plays no part in his late, incomplete dialogue between a philosopher, a Jew (a legalist but hardly an agonist), and a Christian (*Dialogus inter Philosophum, Judaeum et Christianum*).

AESCHYLUS—When accused of revealing the mysteries, he may—like other distracted scribes—have won his acquittal by replying: "I said the first thing that occurred to me—I did not know it was a secret." See *Smyrna*.

AGRI DAGI—the Turkish name for Ararat.

AGRIGENTUM—When Pindar began the Pythian Twelve with his praise of Agrigentum ("fairest city of the mortals, home of Proserpine"), not unlike the pindarites, he had never seen that city. Unlike them, however, he was to see its walls—some fourteen years after his Pythian Twelve. See *Proserpine*.

AKIVA—Rabbi ("Rav" in the Maxioms) Akiva ben Joseph (*c.* 50–135 C.E.). An illiterate who learned the alphabet together with his son, he became "one of the fathers of the world" (Palestinian Talmud, *Shekalim* ["Shekels"], 3:1, 47b). His agon with Rav Ishmael centers on Akiva's allowing for no superfluities in the written Law of the Bible. For Akiva extracted something from every part of speech—not only those that had been glossed by his teacher, Rabbi Nahum of Gimzo. From each repetition of a word, from the joining of the absolute infinitive to the finite forms of the verb, and from the conjunctions "and" or "or"—he read a *ribui* ("extension") of the Law; and from demonstrative pronouns, definite articles, personal pronouns added to a verb, pronomial suffixes or synonymic nouns or verbs—he read a *miyut* ("limitation") of the Law. After the defeat of Bar Kochba, whom Akiva had supported in his revolt against the Romans, Akiva was imprisoned at Caesarea for defying the Roman edict against the teaching of the Torah. Later he was tortured to death, flayed with combs of iron. See *Ishmael* and *Song of Songs*.

AL-MUHARRAM—first month of the Mohammedan year; much envied by metamorphosists, for—since Mohammed's prohibition of intercalary months —al-Muharram no longer introduces the winter half of the year, but moves through all the seasons.

ANABATIC—See *catabatic* and *Proserpine*.

ANAGRAM—See *anaphone, dobut, Heshvan, hypogram, Sète, thrut,* and *Venus.*

ANALOGISTS—Following Aftersong 7, these Scoriae sometimes refer to them as "the sedentaries."

ANAPHONE—used—in the Scoriae—for the phonetic equivalent of an anagram (see *Sète*), though of course a perfect anaphone *may* also be a perfect anagram; but used in Geneva (see *hypogram*) for what the Scoriae call an approximate, para-, or imperfect anagram. Also see *Venus.*

ARARAT—imprudently linked by the melanous merchant to the English "arête," a sharp-crested ridge in rugged mountains (from French *arête,* a fish-bone, from LL *arista,* from the Latin for the blade-shaped ear of corn). It was the periodical *Der Ararat* that had a special Paul Klee issue in 1920, where Klee's "Angelus Novus," later obtained by Walter Benjamin, was listed but not re-produced. That angel may—some scoriasts say—be kin to the cherubin of the Second Finding/Maxiom 15.

ASHKENAZI—See *Proserpine* and *Sephardi.*

ASIE—invoked by Ravel three times at the beginning of *Shéhérazade,* his setting of a three-poem sequence by Tristan Klingsor. "*Asie*," the first of Klingsor's titles (its vowels were sung most hauntingly by Jeanne Hatto, the soprano in the first performance in 1904), was later used as a title by Velimir Chlebnikov. Klingsor never mentions Smyrna, but he does foreshadow the need for cesura-songs with "*interrompre le conte avec art.*" See *cesurasongs, consonants, Humanistan, Leibniz.*

AVERROES—Abū'l-Walīd Mohammed Ibn Ahmad Ibn Rushd (1126–1198); like Maimonides, born in Cordova; next to Maimonides, the most important influence on late medieval Jewish philosophy; linked to Maimonides in the letter of Maimonides to the latter's disciple, Joseph ben Judah. But for signifi-cant contrasts between his work and Maimonides', see Shlomo Pines's "Trans-lator's Introduction" in his English edition of *The Guide of the Perplexed* (Chicago, 1963).

Most memorable for metamorphosists is Léon Gauthier's version, in *Ibn Rochd (Averroès)* (Paris, 1948), of the Judeo-Hispanic-Latin transformation of the Arabic *Ibn Rochd* (the French transliteration of Ibn Rushd) into *Averroes.* Toward the middle of the twelfth century, translations into Latin of Arabic works in Spain were generally the product of a collaboration between a

Christian cleric ignorant of Arabic and a Spanish Jew ignorant of Latin. The Jew, reading aloud, would translate each word or phrase into Spanish; the cleric, in his turn, would translate the Spanish into Latin. Thus, reading aloud the Arabic *Ibn*, the Jew pronounced it like its Hebrew equivalent *Aben* (or more correctly—sciolists say—*Ben*). The Spanish *b* inclined to *v*: thus, *Aven Rochd*, and with "*assimilation consonantique*," *Averrochd*. The cleric replaced the *ch* "*chuintant*" (not to be confused with the *ch* of Chelm), which he sought in vain in Latin, with an *s* "*sifflant*," producing *Averrosd*. Finally, the distaste of Latin for conjoined *s* and *d*, and the need of Latin for a desinence that might be declined, led to the fall of the *d* and the substitution of *es* (or sometimes *is*) for *s*, and the nominative *Averroes*, the accusative *Averroem*, the genitive *Averrois*, the dative *Averroi*, and the ablative *Averroe*. For other metamorphoses, see the fate of *lagerstroemia* in Aftersong 3, and the entries under *thrut* and *dobut*.

AXIOMS—Sciolists insist that Giambattista Vico had already coupled axioms and maxims in his *Autobiografia*: ". . . *aveva già incominciato a . . . ragionar de' particolari per assiomi o sien massime* . . ." But nowhere does he mention maxioms.

*

BABYLONIA—See *Sura*.

BASHI-BAZOUK—equivalent—in Smyrna—of a berserker, from *bazi* "head" and *bozuk* "berserk." Also muttered as an adjective.

BAYADERE—Six sciolists of Smyrna—gone bashi-bazouk—invoke Bouvard and Pécuchet's examination of Fourierism, in which "*pour les célibataires, le Bayadèrisme est institué*"; six other sciolists invoke Goethe's "*Der Gott und die Bajadere*." But the bayadere of the Maxioms is simply a garment woven with horizontal stripes of unequivocal colors: green and gold and azure.

BESHT—acronym for Baal Shem Tov, "Possessor of the Good Name," Israel ben Eliezer, the founder of modern Hasidism, who was born at Okop in Podolia about 1700 and died in 1760. See the early source, *Sefer Shivche ha-Besht* ("The Book of the Praises of the Besht") (Khpust and Berdichev, 1814–15). See *Carpathians*.

BLESSINGS—The tractate *Berachoth* ("Blessings" or "Benedictions") is the first of the eleven tractates of *Zeraim* ("Seeds"), the first of the six *Sedarim* ("Orders") into which the sixty-three tractates of the Mishnah are grouped.

Blessings, however, is the only tractate of that Order which is commented on in the Babylonian Talmud, though the Palestinian Talmud comments on all eleven. See *citron, Oral Law, Sura, seed*.

*

CARPATHIANS—lone mountains that sheltered the Besht and his second wife, Hannah, in the years immediately after their marriage. There (for seven years, some say) he dug—she carted—clay. See *Besht*.

CATABATIC—See *katabasis*.

CESURASONGS—For cesura as *gegenrhythmische Unterbrechung*—counter-rhythmic suspension—pindarites still ponder Hölderlin's *Anmerkungen zum Oedipus* and his *Anmerkungen zur Antigonae*. Also see *Asie* (and for the *Grus Antigone*, see *crane*).

CHELM—The Chelm of revehent time—resistant to metamorphosis—was a town southeast of Lublin in Poland. On November 6, 1942, almost all of its Jews—including 2,000 Jews who had been deported there from Slovakia—were deported by the Germans to Sobibor for extermination. Fifteen survived at the liberation of Chelm on July 22, 1944. For the Chelm of the fatuists, see the entry under *Sefer ha-Bedicha*.

CHIBOUQUE—the Turkish *chibuk*, a long tobacco pipe of the kind the melanous merchant puffed in Smyrna. Metamorphosists note its appearance in English as "chibouk," "chibbok," and "chiboque," in addition to the "chibouque" of the Maxioms; but this latter spelling accords with both Byron in *The Corsair* and Disraeli in *Tancred* (though Morier in *Ayesha* uses "chibouk" as his base for: "The end of the room was crowded with chiboukchies or pipe-men").

CITRON—"He who sees a citron in his dreams is comely before his Maker, for it is said 'you shall take the fruit of a comely tree.'" So reads *Berachoth* 57a on the citron used—together with branches of palm trees, boughs of myrtle, and willows of the brook—in celebrating the Feast of Harvest or Tabernacles (the Hebrew *Sukkoth*). See Third Finding/Maxiom 8.

CLOUDS—Some say that only trivial metamorphosists pursue cloud reveries to the accompaniment of the first of Debussy's *Nocturnes*; or with the aid of Luke Howard's essay "On the Modifications of Clouds" (London, 1803) or of Goethe's interest in Howard in his *Naturwissenschaftliche Schriften*; or of his poetic "*Trilogie zu Howards Wolkenlehre*," especially "*Howards Ehrengedächtnis*," with its sections, "*Stratus*," "*Kumulus*," "*Cirrus*," and "*Nimbus*"; or of Ruskin's *The Storm Cloud of the Nineteenth Century* (Orpington, 1884). And those who so assert point out that Flaubert's copy of Howard, borrowed from the Bibliothèque Nationale, only served him for *Bouvard et Pécuchet*: "*Pour se connaître aux signes du temps, ils étudièrent les nuages d'après la classification de Luke-Howard. Ils contemplaient ceux qui s'allongent comme des crinières, ceux qui ressemblent à des îles, ceux qu'on prendrait pour des montagnes de neige, tâchant de distinguer les nimbus des cirrus, les stratus des cumulus; les formes changeaient avant qu'ils eussent trouvé les noms*"—a fleeting terminus. But see *Kant*.

CONSONANTS—In Aftersong 6, among the "scribes who savor consonants," sciolists list not only one who was distant from Chelm, Velimir Chlebnikov (who scorned vowels as the "feminine element of language," fit only for "linking masculine sounds"), but Mandelstam himself: "The word reproduces itself, not through vowels, but through consonants. The consonants are the *seed* and the assurance of posterity of language. The atrophy of the sense of the consonant is evidence of enfeebled linguistic awareness." Against the consonantists, one resolute vowelist is Anne Pierre Jacques de Vismes (1745–1819), who, in *Pasilogie; ou, De la Musique, Considérée comme Langue Universelle* (Paris, 1806), even as he proposes an enharmonic international alphabet of twenty-one letters, makes clear the relationship between letters—*especially vowels*—and the musical scales used in antiquity. Also see *Asie, Humanistan*, and *seed*.

COOK, CAPTAIN JAMES—Despite the Fourth Finding/Maxiom 8, J.C. Beaglehole, the editor of Cook's journals, in enumerating the livestock presented by Cook in 1777 to "Paulaho, his host at Tongatapu, the Tu'i Tonga himself, the massive sacred king" is careful to explain the *omission* of "the tortoise, often called 'Captain Cook's Tortoise,' and said to be from the Galapagos, who used to roam the palace grounds at Nuko 'alofa," noting of that tacit tortoise, who "died, internationally noticed, in May 1966," that "it seems much more likely that the tortoise landed in Tonga under later auspices." As the entry under *Galapagos* allows us to infer, even those Tongans who rashly identified a Galapagan tortoise as Captain Cook's never implied that he had brought it from Galapagos but from the Thames—which it had reached by means other than Cook.

COUNTERMAXIOMS—Paul-Jean Toulet (1867–1920) was perhaps indebted to them for the title of his posthumous 1921 volume, *Contrerimes*; but where he was given to quatrains, neither the maxioms nor the countermaxioms are. See *tercets*.

CRANE—identified by some as the *Grus communis*, though they note that the Common Crane is no less complex than is *sensus communis* (witness the role of common sense in Kant's *Critique of Aesthetic Judgement*). Analogists refer, for the hoarse savant on the "candid back" of a crane, to Chikuden of the nineteenth-century Nanga School, with his predilection for the *Grus (Pseudogeranus) leucauchen*, the Tan-cho Crane, bearer of savants on its back to the Isle of the Immortals; while others murmur that both the Common Crane and Tan-cho Crane are grey—the candid back must surely belong to *Grus (Sarcogeranus) leucogeranus*, the Asiatic White Crane, which does range—at certain seasons—as far north as Chelm. Indeed six pindarites identify that as the crane of Schiller's "*Die Kraniche des Ibykus*," though five others opt for the *Grus Antigone*, the Antique Crane. In any case, all agree that its iris is generally crimson, orange, or yellow. Also see *cesurasongs* and *isosceles*.

*

DAVID—For the night, the northwind, and the lyre that hung above the bed of the sleeping psalmist (First Finding/Maxiom 6 and Sixth Finding/"The Song of Song"), see *Berachoth* 3b.

DARWIN—See *Galapagos* and *Kent*.

DEL MEDIGO, JOSEPH SOLOMON—Born in Candia, Crete, in 1591, Del Medigo traversed rabbinics, medicine, astronomy, mathematics, chemistry, mechanics, geography, logic, metaphysics, ethics, and much of the Diaspora: Padua, where he studied with Galileo and Cremonini; Cairo; Constantinople; Poland; Rumania; Vilna; Hamburg; Amsterdam; Frankfurt am Main; Prague, where he died in 1655. In Amsterdam, where Del Medigo served as rabbi from 1626 to 1629, he wrote his *Sefer Elim* ("Book of Elim," from the Elim of Exodus 15:27, where there were twelve fountains or wells and seventy palm trees). In it he replied to the queries of the Lithuanian Karaite, Zerach bar Nathan. The rabbis prohibited the printing of his full text; and the amputated version was published by Manasseh ben Israel in 1629 (the full text waited for Abraham Geiger in 1840). In 1677 this version appeared in quarto as the thirty-first item in the library of Spinoza under the title of *Een Rabbinsch Mathematisch Boeck*. (That same library also included *Bechinat ha-Dat*—"The Examination of Religion"—by Del Medigo's fifteenth-century forebear on his mother's side, Elijah ben Moses Abba Del Medigo of Crete, the ardent

Averroist, friend of Pico della Mirandola, and anti-kabalist, who headed the yeshiva at Padua for a time.) Aftersong 11 reaches, however, for what Spinoza may well have read of the unexpurgated version. He may also have seen Del Medigo's *Taalumot Chochma* (1629–1631), a collection of kabalistic treatises that contains a central source for the legends of the life of Luria: three letters written to a friend in Cracow by Shlomel Dresnitz, an immigrant to Safed from Moravia. See *Averroes, Galileo, Luria,* and *Zerach bar Nathan.*

DENEB—otherwise known as *Arided, Os rosae, Rosemund, Uropygium, Aridif, Arrioph, Gallina, Al Dhanab al Dajājah, Denebadigege, Denebedigege,* or *Deneb Adige.* Because of this onomastic variety, Deneb is dear to metamorphosists, despite its brilliant, constant whiteness (and their own love of chiaroscuro).

DOBUT—Doubt is bartered for dobut (Third Finding/Maxiom 3) through the exchange of two letters. See *thrut.*

＊

ECCLESIASTESISTS—See *kohelethites.*

EEN RABBINSCH MATHEMATISCH BOECK—See *Del Medigo.*

ELEVEN—See—under *Blessings*—the number of tractates in *Zeraim* ("Seeds"), the first *Seder* ("Order") of the Mishnah.

EMANCIPATION—Portuguese Jews became full citizens in France in 1790, and all Jews in 1791; Holland gave Jews full citizenship in 1796; Switzerland in 1866; Austria in 1868.

FARMINGTON—See *the the.*

FATUIST—derived from *ignis fatuus.* Like the scribes, pinarites, galimatiasists, amphibolists, scoriasts, and sciolists, the fatuists are never listed as a separate tribe; they may be found in at least ten of the eleven sects.

FEAST OF HARVEST—See *citron.*

FLAMMANTIA MOENIA MUNDI—In crossing the "flaming walls of the world," the perfect woman may well have drawn not only on Lucretius but on a Lucretian echo in Pica della Mirandola. For though Pico himself is aware of his own deficiencies as a poet (on October 16, 1486, he writes to a friend:

[153]

"*Rythmos meas non est quod desideres*"), his Latin elegiacs entitled *Ad Deum deprecatoria* might well have compelled her attention—with their "*super excelsi flammantia moenia mundi.*" See *Del Medigo*.

*

GALAPAGOS—visited by the *Beagle* and Darwin in 1835, by the *Acushnet* and Melville in 1841, and—despite the fatuists' Fourth Finding/Maxiom 8—never visited by Cook.

GALILEO—See *Venus* and—for one of Galileo's students—*Del Medigo*.

GALIMATIAS—Some say—agreeing with Littré—that it was Boileau who first distinguished between the simple galimatias, which is not understood by its hearers, and the double galimatias, "*où l'auteur ne se comprend pas lui-même.*"

GALIMATIASISTS—derived their name from *galimatias*. See *sciolists*.

GELA—See *Smyrna*.

GESTRUEMIA—See *Lagerstroem*.

GIUDICI, GIOVANNI—the "poet from Milan" (Fifth Finding/Maxiom 3 and Aftersong 23), where he has lived since 1958, was born in Le Grazie in 1924. See *La vita in versi* (1968), *Autobiologia* (1969), and *O beatrice* (1972).

GONIUM—Protozoa of this kind—with their preference for tranquil fresh waters—are especially common near lakeside quays or listless paralimnions.

*

HALLUCINARIUM—For some of its inhabitants, see the entry under *hypogram*. Its name—some fatuists say—was derived in opposition to *Elucidarium*, a title used by Honoré d'Autun (pseudonym, Augustodunensis). For one of Saadya Gaon's few entries into the hallucinarium, see the entry under his name.

HAPHAZARD—In the text from *The Guide of the Perplexed* that appears as epigraph for these Scoriae, the haphazard is excluded by Maimonides; yet—earlier—he had said: "Hence you should not ask of me here anything beyond the chapter headings. And even those are not set down in order or arranged in coherent fashion . . . but rather are scattered and entangled with other subjects that are to be clarified." Only the misguided will find a contradiction.

HESHVAN—In his Preface to the Maxioms, the hoarse savant dismembers as two words, *mar* and *Heshvan*, what sciolists know as a single word: *Marheshvan*, derived from the Babylonian *Ara-ah-shamnu*, meaning eighth month (which it is for the Jewish religious year, beginning with Nisan, though it is the second month for the civil year, beginning with Tishri). Radak (acronym for Rabbi David Kimchi, the thirteenth-century grammarian and commentator of Narbonne) saw *Marheshvan* as transposed from (*y)erah/shimon* ("the eighth month")—more evident as a para-anagram in untransliterated Hebrew. Though some agree with the hoarse savant's two-word reading, they gloss the *mar* not as "bitter" but as the homonymic *mar* meaning "sir, mister, *signore*" to allow this month—in compensation for its lack of feast-days—a title no other month receives. But the gloss of the hoarse savant does have a bitter justification: the German Kristallnacht of November 9/10th, 1938, took place on the 15/16th of Heshvan.

HUMANISTAN—a site (Fifth Finding/Maxiom 1) first identified by Velimir Chlebnikov (1885–1922) in *Ladomir*, his most pensive poem. The name *may* have reached Chelm by way of Mandelstam, for it was he who said of Chlebnikov: "He was like a mole, who excavates underground galleries for the future."

HYPOGRAM—For hypograms, anagrams, anaphones, paragrams, mannequins, paramorphs, and the *Corpus paramorphicum*, see the eight boxes in the Bibliothèque Publique et Universitaire de Genève, with their 115 notebooks and additional loose papers of Ferdinand de Saussure (*Mss. fr. 3962–3969*, dating from 1906 to 1909). Some say that listless lakeside lecterns and quays (in Geneva, Orta S. Giulio, Chelm) are given to more—and more hectic dismembering of—phemes than are the quays and lecterns that overlook already restless seas. See *isosceles*.

*

ISAR—river that flows through Munich, city whose chief synagogue was destroyed on July 8, 1938.

ISHMAEL—Rabbi ("Rav" in the Maxioms) Ishmael ben Elisha, friend and agonist of Akiva, insisted that "the Torah spoke in the language of the sons of men" (*Kerithoth*, ["Excisions"] 11a—and elsewhere); i.e., each pleonasm or redundancy was not to be read in Akiva's way, as if it carried precise or meditated weight in determining the Law. This dictum of Ishmael supported his expansion of Hillel's seven hermeneutic rules into The Thirteen Rules, the fundamental map for all talmudic legal exegesis, charting the ways of: a fortiori inferences from major to minor and minor to major; exegetical, constructional, and exorbitant analogies; generalization and particularization; contextual explanation; juxtaposition; refutation; reinstatement; modification (see Second Finding/Maxiom 12). Maimonides "misunderstood" Ishmael's dictum (Second Finding/Maxiom 9): he calls on it as an anti-literal antidote against anthropomorphic infiltrations into "the imagination of the multitude" (*The Guide of the Perplexed*, I, 26)—an intent very different from Ishmael's. See *Akiva*.

ISOSCELES—For the "white isosceles" of the cranes in the First Finding/ Maxiom 5, six sciolists cite Buffon: "*Les grues portent leur vol très-haut, et se mettent en ordre pour voyager; elles forment un triangle à peu près isocèle, comme pour fendre l'air plus aisement.*" But pindarites point to Palamedes, inventor—some say—of the Greek alphabet, to whom the triangular flight of the crane suggested the Greek upsilon (Latin *v*, first letter of *ver*, "spring"—see Martial, IX, 13); though others—glossing Lucan's reference to Palamedes—say it suggested the Greek capital lambda, and still others—see below—say it was the capital delta. These same pindarites note that, in a notebook in Geneva (*Ms. fr. 3965*; see *hypogram*), de Saussure had firmly framed in blue and red pencil both the text and Panckoucke's translation of another epigram of Martial (XIII, 75) on the crane as the bird of Palamedes: "*GRUES: Turbabis versus nec littera tota volabit/ Unam perdideris si Palamedis avem* (*Trad. Panckoucke: Tu dérangeras le triangle, et le delta ne sera plus entier au sein des airs si tu en ôtes un seul des oiseaux de Palamède*)"; and above this, still within the blue and red frame, de Saussure had inscribed in capitals: "*ALLUSION A L'HYPOGRAMME EN TANT QU'HYPOGRAMME?*"—as if to say: if you disorder—in the least way—the mode in which the scribe has distributed the dismembered letters of a central word through his text, the message will be lost. (And amphibolists remind us that, in that same epigram of Martial, W.C.A. Ker had found two meanings in *versus*, "line.") Also see *crane*.

IZMIR—name to which Smyrna has veered—though the Third Finding/ Maxiom 3 reverses that movement.

*

JEJUNUM—Sciolists, following Arthur W. Ham's *Histology*, note that: "The villi of the duodenum are broader than those elsewhere, and many examples of leaf-like ones can be found in this region. In the upper part of the jejunum, the villi, in general, are said to be tongue-shaped."

*

KABALIST—Had he (Second Finding/Maxiom 14) been enlightened by Joseph Gikatila, Menachem Recanati, or Todros ben Joseph Abulafia? By Isaac ben Latif, Abraham ben Isaac of Gerona, or Rabbi Isaac the Blind? By Moses Cordovero, Yehuda Chayyat, or Luria himself? And if his light was Luria, which of the nine transmitters did he follow: Chayim Vital, Samuel Vital, or Joseph ibn Tabul? Moses Jonah of Safed, Israel Saruk, or Moses Najara? Judah Mishan, Joseph Arzin, or Gedaliah ha-Levi? Or did he—through the lens of nine on nine—divine one point of origin? For fuller word on *point*, see the entry under *seed*. Also see *Luria*.

KANT—In "The Perfect Woman Reads A Page of Kant," the page she reads may—some sciolists say—be in the *Metaphysische Anfangsgründe der Tugendlehre*, the second part of the *Metaphysik der Sitten*; but the sentence, *"nur die Höllenfahrt des Selbsterkenntnisses bahnt den Weg zur Vergötterung,"* woven into the first stanza, was parenthesized by Kant and had been borrowed by him—with minor changes—from Johann Georg Hamann (in his *"Abelardi Virbii Chimärische Einfälle"*); yet the perfect woman may well have read another page, in the *Streit der Fakultäten*, where Kant borrowed Hamann's sentence again, with minor changes but in quotation marks and with explicit mention of Hamann's name. But for the final word of her meditation, "regret," all sciolists agree that she must have remembered still another page—from the *Kritik der Urteilskraft*: "Apart from some such antinomy reason could never bring itself to . . . submit to sacrifices involving the complete dissipation of so many otherwise brilliant hopes. . . . It is not without a pang of regret that it appears to part company with these hopes. . . ." For Kant, cloud-devoted metamorphosists rely on C.F. Reusch and add: On the day of Kant's death, February 12, 1804, a soldier who—from the bridge in Königsberg—had noted a light, small cloud in the azure sky of a rare day, identified that cloud as the soul of Kant on its way to heaven.

KARAITES—principal anti-rabbinite sect in the history of Judaism, surfacing in the eighth century as followers of Anan ben David and taking their name, *Karaim, Baalei ha-Mikra* ("People of the Scriptures") in the ninth century;

their later life—sometimes flowering, more often dwindling—traverses the Persian borderlands, Babylonia, Egypt, Palestine, Byzantium, the Crimea, and Lithuania. Their tenets seemed to hold fast to the Written Law of the Bible, denying the weight of the Oral Law, redacted in the Talmud; but for Zvi Ankori (*Karaites in Byzantium*, New York and Jerusalem, 1959, p. 17): "Anan's widely heralded fundamentalism and exclusive reliance on the letter of the Written Law are largely a misnomer. Rather, his was an *ex post facto* attempt to *read into the Bible* (the full twenty-four volumes of it and not the Pentateuch alone) the customs and observances already practiced by the sectarians." At times both karaite and rabbinite were given to rapprochement, and recent events in Israel have confirmed that desire. See *Oral Law* and *Zerach bar Nathan*.

KATABASIS—Where anabasis is ascent or advance and anabatic is ascending or advancing, katabasis is descent or retreat and katabatic (or catabatic, in the Maxioms) is descending or retreating. De Quincey uses the antonyms in the second of their two senses: "The Russian anabasis and katabasis of Napoleon." But the agonists of the Maxioms contrast them in their first sense alone, as ascent and descent, or ascending and descending. For Maimonides on "descending" and "ascending," see *The Guide of the Perplexed*, I, 10. Also see *Proserpine*.

KENT—Though Darwin was born at Shrewsbury (in 1809), from 1842 until his death in 1882 he lived in the village of Down in Kent.

KOHELETHITES—This earlier name for the ecclesiastesists derives from *Koheleth*, the Hebrew name for Ecclesiastes. Maimonides—though hardly an ecclesiastesist—does defend *Koheleth* against the charge reported in the *Midrash Leviticus Rabbah*, XXVIII: "[Some] wanted to suppress the book of Ecclesiastes because its words incline to those of the heretics," by distinguishing between the eternity a parte post and the eternity a parte ante of the world (*The Guide of the Perplexed*, II, 28). Pascal, who twice cites *Midrash Koheleth* in his *Pensées*, 446 (Lafuma, 537), might well have been in partial sympathy with them under either name. (To which sciolists add that while Pascal transliterated the Hebrew as *Misdrach el Kohelet*, Pico della Mirandola uses *Midras cöeleth* in his *Apologia*). See *flammantia moenia mundi*.

KRIEGEL, FRANTISEK—a Jewish Czech physician, born in Poland, Chairman of the National Front in the post-January-1968 Czech government and member of the Dubcek delegation to Moscow in 1968; the "Galician Jew" of the quotation—reliably attributed to Leonid Brezhnev—with which the Fifth

Finding/Maxiom 11 begins. At the May 1969 Plenum, Kriegel was expelled from the party on charges of being antiparty, antisocialist, and anti-Soviet.

*

LAGERSTROEM, MAGNUS—Though Aftersong 3 traces the roots of the gestruemia to the lagerstroemia, the tree named by Linnaeus for Herr Magnus Lagerstroem, it fails to add that Lagerstroem himself was from Gottenburg, and that the gestruemia celebrated in the Maxioms—with flowers produced in panicles that are at first pale rose-colored, then gradually heighten to "mauve extravagance"—was not *elegans, grandiflora, indica, rosea, parviflora, speciosa,* or *tomentosa,* but stemmed from the *lagerstroemia reginae.*

LEIBNIZ—For Chlebnikov's "frequent conversations with the $\sqrt{-1}$ of Leibniz," see the former's "His Own Domain" (written in 1919 as a possible preface to his collected works). Also see *pandoche* and *Spinoza.*

LEVI, MARIO—a Turinese physician who—together with his son, Roberto, and wife, Teresa—had taken refuge in Orta S. Giulio during World War II. At about seven o'clock on the evening of September 15, 1943—a week after the armistice between the Italian government and the Allies—two trucks of S.S. troops arrived on the main square of Orta S. Giulio, site of the town hall. One of the municipal employees immediately alerted a friend of the Levis, who hurried off to alert Roberto Levi. But half-an-hour later the S.S. were seen carrying away both father and son in one of the trucks. Their end is uncertain —but very probably they joined a group of fifteen to twenty Jews who were captured in the area of Lake Maggiore, shot by the Germans, then cast into the lake.

LEVINAS, EMMANUEL—born in Kovno, Lithuania, in 1905; in France since 1923. In Gatesong 5 and Fifth Finding/Maxiom 7, the Maxioms do not inter- sect his *Difficile liberté: Essais sur le judaïsme* (Paris, 1963) or his *Quatre lectures talmudiques* (Paris, 1968), but *"Le Dit et le dire"* (*Le Nouveau Commerce,* XVIII- XIX, Printemps 1971, pp. 19–48).

LURIA, ISAAC BEN SOLOMON—Born—of an Ashkenazi father and a Sephardi mother—in Jerusalem in 1534, but raised in Egypt. During his stay there he lived some seven years (though others—see the Second Finding/Maxiom 14— hint at thirteen years) on Jazīrat al-Rawda, an island in the Nile. About 1569 he settled in Safed, where he died in 1572. Shortly after his death, his disciple

Chayim Vital, son of an immigrant from Calabria, transcribed/expanded Luria's kabalistic teachings in *Etz Chayim* ("The Tree of Life"), consisting of eight parts, called Gates. To these initial eight Gates, Vital's son Samuel added eight more in his compilation, *Shemoneh Shearim* ("The Eight Gates"). For seven other transmitters of Luria's teachings, see *kabalist*; and for a biographical source for Luria's life, see the entry under *Del Medigo*.

✳

MACHIAVELLI—Six say that "a trenchant look at . . . [his] fine arts" (Fourth Finding/Maxiom 2) is best abetted by Claude Lefort, *Le Travail de l'oeuvre: Machiavel*. But six insist that—to that end—the lens of the late Leo Strauss is still the sharpest.

MAIANDROS—See *Menderes*.

MAIMONIDES—Moses ben Maimon (known also as the Rambam, acronym for Rabbi Moses ben Maimon) was born in Cordova in 1135 and died in Egypt or Palestine in 1204. The most lucid jurist and most subtle philosopher produced by the post-talmudic Diaspora, his central texts are two: the *Mishneh Torah* ("Re-presentation of the Torah")—his only principal work in Hebrew —and his *Guide of the Perplexed*. For an agonistic view of the relation between Maimonides as legalist and as philosopher, see Leo Strauss's "Introductory Essay" in Shlomo Pines's edition of the *Guide* (Chicago, 1963); and for a more holistic wedding of philosophy and the Oral Law in Maimonides, see Isadore Twersky, "Aspects of the Mishneh Torah," in *Jewish Medieval and Renaissance Studies*, ed. A. Altmann (Cambridge, 1967), with its careful analysis of "the crushing literalism" in Maimonides' idiosyncratic use as proof text of a talmudic comment in praise of Jochanan ben Zakkai: "He did not leave [unstudied] Scripture, Mishnah, Gemara, Halakah, Haggada, details of the Torah, details of the Scribes, inferences *a minori ad majus*, analogies, calendrical computations, gematriot, the speech of the Ministering Angels, the speech of spirits, and the speech of palm-trees, fullers' parables and fox fables, great matters or small matters. '*Great matters*' mean the *ma'aseh merkabah* [identified by Maimonides with metaphysics], 'small matters,' the discussions of Abbaye and Rabba." (*Sukkah* 28a and *Baba Batra* ["The Last Gate"] 134a—but the order of the items differs in the two texts). See *Averroes, haphazard, Ishmael, katabasis, kohelethites, Oral Law, particular,* and *precision*.

MALBIM—acronym for Meir Loeb ben Jechiel Michael (1809–1879), biblical commentator, clarifier—in 613 paragraphs, 248 on linguistic usage and 365 in explanation of verbs and synonyms—of the methods of biblical exegesis. Cited under *pearls*.

MANDELSTAM—See *Smyrna, Sephardi, Underwood, Proserpine,* and *Humanistan*.

MAXIMS—See *axioms*.

MAXIOMS—See *axioms*.

MENDERES—the modern (Turkish) name for the river Maiandros or Maeander.

MISHNAH—See *Oral Law* and *seed*.

MNEMOSYNE—To ease the throb and thraw of failed recall or—some say—of too sharp recall, the victims of Mnemosyne still call on ancient opiates: Johann Host von Rombcrch's *Congestiorum Artificiose Memorie* (Venice, 1520), Jacopo Publico's *Ars Memorativa* (Cologne, 1480), and Cosmas Rosselius's *Thesavrvs Artificiosae Memoriae* (Venice, 1579). But some alter the order of these palliatives, beginning with Rosselius—to try their hands at his digital signs.

MOULOUD MAMMERI—See *Si Mohand-ou-Mhand*.

*

NENUPHAR—Littré corrects Scheler's view of nenuphar—relayed by restless sedentaries—as irregularly derived from *nymphaea,* the Latin and Greek for water lily: its proper stem is the Persian *noûfer, niloûfer*. These same sedentaries, noting the Bengali line, "nenuphar/ where the heart's idol dwelt," by a late follower of Chandidās and bearer of his name, point to the *Sahaja* movement's sixty-four types of *Nayikās,* the women of love (eight main types, each subdivided into eight subsidiary types), as adumbrations of the perfect woman. But even fatuists can see that only half of these types foreshadow her in any way.

NOTITIA OPTICAE PROMOTAE—See *pandoche*.

*

ORAL LAW—"One should always divide his years into three: a third to Mikra [the Bible], a third to Mishnah, and a third to Talmud" (*Kiddushin* ["Betrothals"] 30a). The Mikra is the Written Law; the Mishnah, the first stage of the

Oral Law to be redacted, passing the Gate of Text in Palestine in the third century C.E.; while for the two redactions of the Talmud (that is, the addition of the Gemara—the second stage of the Oral Law—to the Mishnah), see the entries under *Sura* and *seed*. But for Maimonides' intricate gloss on this passage and his view of the Talmud as the "ever expanding commentary on the Mishnah," see the same essay by Isadore Twersky cited under *Maimonides*. Also see *karaites*.

ORIGEN—For Origen on auto-castration (though with no direct mention of yataghan), six sciolists refer to his *Comment. in Matthaeum Tomus XV* on Matthew 19:12 in the section "*De differentia eunuchorum*" (Migne, P.G., Vol. 13). Eusebius sees in Origen's own auto-castration a demonstration of his zeal, but —as Eugène de Faye notes—"*il reconnait que ce zèle était intempestif.*" For his own plight at the hands of Fulbert's thugs, Abelard—in his *Historia Calamitatum* (Migne, *P.L.*, Vol. 178, col. 177)—recalls the act of Origen. See *Abelard* and *yataghan*.

ORTA S. GIULIO—Its distance from Chelm has never been calculated, but it is not incalculable.

*

PANDOCHE—In his *Notitia opticae promotae* (a two-page document published in Frankfurt in 1671), Leibniz treats of a defect common to ordinary lenses and of the superiority of the lenses he called *pandoches* (Aftersong 9): "*Lentes pandochae colligunt omnes radios in unam lineam*"—a claim rather hard to follow in what follows, and Spinoza regrets his inability to do so in his letter to Leibniz of November 9, 1671 ("*Doleo, quod mentem tuam, quam tamen credo te satis clare exposuisse, non satis assequi potuerim*"—*Epistola* XLVI).

PARMIGIANINO—devoted to the cadence of the neck, but much less devoted to clouds—and thus less dear to metamorphosists—than Correggio, for whom the metamorphosists most often consult Hubert Damisch, *Théorie du /nuage/* (Paris, 1972).

PARTICULAR—For "the fate of that particular" in "The Ayre of the Rhomboid Fountain," the sedentaries sometimes cite Maimonides on particularization (*The Guide of the Perplexed* I, 74; II, 21; and elsewhere).

PEARLS—"The Lied of Yet" remembers Proverbs 31:10, but where some read, "who can find a virtuous (or 'valiant') woman, her worth is far above rubies," others translate "pearls," still others "jewels," and the Malbim notes, as another possible meaning for the Hebrew *michrah*, not "worth" but "place"—that is, her dwelling is even more distant than pearls, which are most dearly sought and sought afar. See *Malbim.*

PHLEGM—For phlegm that differs from the phlegm of the First Finding/ Maxiom 27, see Nietzsche's bitter remedy: "*Phlegmatische naturen sind nur so zu begeistern, dass man sie fanatisiert*" (*Morgenröte*, IV Buch, 222). "The only way to bestir phlegmatic temperaments is to make them fanatics."

PINARITES—See *pinarium*, from which the pinarites derive their name. Only fatuists confound them with the pindarites.

PINARIUM—term in Parisian argot for a *pièce où on fait l'amour.* Some say it entered the Scoriae by way of Smyrna and note its absence from Raphael Levy's *Contribution à la lexicographie française selon d'anciens textes d'origine juive* (Syracuse, 1960).

PINDARITES—Perhaps their first forebear was Philo the Jew of Alexandria, who, in his *De Providentia*, cites Pindar's paean on the eclipse of February 16 or 17 in 478, or that of April 30, 463. But galimatiasists remind us that the *De Providentia* itself is only known to us in full in an Armenian translation: Eusebius transmitted substantial fragments of the Greek—but not the whole. And though Philo refers to his citation in the Eusebian fragments, the citation itself lies under the lens of the Armenian and of Aucher's Latin translation therefrom (1882). But "the Armenian who could manage Philo with general accuracy was unable to tackle Pindar . . . [and] the Latin version in Aucher has enough semblance to show identity, but otherwise is sheer nonsense" (F. H. Colson). To which the sciolists reply: but we *do* have that Pindaric fragment in other—and lucid—transcriptions.

PRECISION—See both the epigraph for the Scoriae, taken from Maimonides, and the entry under *Sète.*

PROSERPINE—Though agonists pit the Proserpine of Mandelstam (see Aftersong 14, transcribed by an elusive Slavist) against the Proserpine of Pindar, catabatic against anabatic, Ashkenazi against Sephardi, devehent against revehent, eternity a parte post against eternity a parte ante, the winterwhite of Petrograd against the almondwhite of Agrigentum, the Gate of Text against the Gate of Talk—no metamorphosist would.

PUMBEDITHA—See *Sura.*

*

RAV AKIVA—See *Akiva.*

RAV ISHMAEL—See *Ishmael.*

RAVEL—See *Asie.*

REDACTIONS—See *Sura.*

REVEHENT—carrying back; antonym of "devehent." See *Proserpine.*

*

SAADYA GAON—Saadya ben Joseph (888–942) was Gaon (head of the academy) of Sura from 928 until his death—though with some quarrelsome interruptions. The most lucid Jewish philosopher and rabbinist of his time (and the principal agonist against the karaites), he only entered the hallucinarium once, with his "*Shir al ha-Otioth*" ("Song on the Letters"—of the alphabet occurring in the Bible): there—for instance—the first of his twenty-eight quatrains begins with the first letter, *aleph,* and uses the numerical value of the initial letters of the following five words to write out 42,377, the number of times the *aleph* occurs in the Bible. As portulan for the song, the commentary after each quatrain (probably by Saadya himself) is—some say—of indispensable help. See *karaites* and *Sura.*

SABBATH QUEEN—When the Sabbath complains that she, as the seventh day, is left outside the pairings, two by two, available to each of the other days, the reply to her is: she too has her "dear match"—the whole of Israel (*Midrash Rabbah* on Genesis, Chapter 11). On greeting her as "queen," see *Shabbat* ("Sabbath") 119a. Also see *tercets.*

SAVANTS—Pinarites—of Smyrna—point to Charles Fourier's *Le nouveau monde amoureux* for the "*incapacité des savants civilisés.*" But neither Mme. Ebauche, Mme. Debauch, Fra Aziman, Frau Conortz, Signora Enthymeme, Greta Lentz, or Gaia Canso—ever seconded that charge. See *pinarites.*

SCIOLISTS—Like the fatuists, amphibolists, pinarites, galimatiasists, scoriasts, and scribes, the sciolists are never listed as a separate sect: they may be found among at least ten of the eleven tribes.

SCORIASTS—men more intent on scoriae than on volcanoes—live or spent— or on an unaddendaed text. Identified—by some—with sciolists.

SEED—"Seeds" (*Zeraim*) is the title of the first of the six Orders (*Sedarim*) into which the sixty-three tractates of the Mishnah are grouped. Of these sixty-three tractates, the Babylonian Talmud has *Gemara*—or commentary—on thirty-seven, the Jerusalem—or better, Palestinian—Talmud on thirty-nine. (But the lacunae are not always for the same tractate: the Palestinian Talmud completely lacks the last two Orders except for one tractate; and the Jerusalem Talmud completely lacks the first, except for one tractate, *Berachoth*.) For the "thread" of Cesurasong 5 ("seed : thread : drum/ : :/ point : line : volume"), some note that the Hebrew for tractate (*Masechta*) is possibly derived from "to weave" and is thus a "web," like the Latin *textus* from *texere*. To which more obsessive analogists—citing Jean Laude—add: "*Les mythes des Dogon laissent apparaître des idées analogues: trois 'paroles' auraient été révelées aux humains. Chacun marque un progrès dans l'ordre de l'invention technique et montre le passage d'une conception de l'espace ponctuel (le point est assimilé à une graine) à celle de l'espace linéaire (le ligne est celle d'un fil de tissage), enfin, à celle de l'espace tridimensionnel (le volume est assimilé au tambour d'aisselle).*" See *Oral Law* and *Sura*.

SEFER HA-BEDICHA (V'HA-CHIDUD)—This "Book of Jest and Wit," by A. Drujanoff (Tel Aviv, 1936), contains (in Volume Two, pp. 1–36, entries 1022 to 1085) an ample repertory of the fatuists' lying legends of Chelm, most often drawn or borrowed from sources whose "lids had never opened on/ the eucalyptus gates of Chelm" (Gatesong 3).

SEME—anglicized—in "The Lied of Yet"—by the perfect woman; from the French *sème*, already noted by J. Marouzeau in 1933 as adopted by "*certaines linguistes*" in place of *semantème* to designate an element of meaning (*Lexique de la terminologie linguistique*, Paris, 1933).

SEMI-UNCIAL—The semi-uncials of the pindarite (Third Finding/Maxiom 13) may be as negligent—and as awkward to read—as the semi-uncial hand of Oxyrhynchus Papyrus No. 408, with its especially mutilated text of a fragment by Pindar, a text so garbled that Aimé Puech is hard pressed to classify it as epinicion, hymn, paean, dithyramb, prosodion, parthenion, hyporchema, eulogy, encomium, or threnody—and labels it simply "*d'origine incertaine.*" The Gate of Text is often in uncertain hands.

SEPHARDI—a descendant of Jews who lived in Spain and Portugal before the expulsion of 1492; from *Sepharad*, the usual Hebrew name for the Iberian peninsula after the eighth century C.E. (the biblical *Sepharad* mentioned in Obadiah 1:20 had originally meant Sardis, the capital of Lydia in Asia Minor—witness E. Littmann's publication of the Aramaic/Greek inscription excavated at Sardis). Some see in the Maxioms' Spinoza a Sephardi in contrast to the Maxioms' Ashkenazi, Mandelstam; but the perfect woman has never drawn such unrefined distinctions. For a more recent evocation of *Sepharad*, see the long Catalan poem by Salvador Espriu (begun at Lavinia in June 1957 and completed at Sinera in July 1958): *La pell de brau*, a work that also calls on the Hebrew *Golah*—Exile.

SÈTE—birth and burial place of Valéry and site of his seaside cemetery; in older spelling, Cette. Both Sète and Cette provide approximate anagrams for Valéry's M. Teste (though—on the phonic side alone—Cette is a perfect anaphone). But for such approximations, Valéry's own preface to his texts on Teste reminds us: "*L'acte d'écrire demande toujours un certain 'sacrifice de l'intellect.' On sait bien, par exemple, que les conditions de la lecture littéraire sont incompatibles avec une précision excessive du langage. . . . Nous ne gagnons les attentions qu'à la faveur de quelque amusement . . .*" Those in the hallucinarium may read his words as a lament over combinatorial imperfections, imprecisions; those—if any—who have escaped the hallucinarium may—more resignedly—see his words as an admonition against the mistaking of "*quelque amusement*" for an adequate act of the intellect.

SEVEN—See *Luria*'s years on an island in the Nile and the years of the *Besht* in the *Carpathians*.

SI MOHAND-OU-MHAND—The Berber poet, chanter of the *Isefra*, who was born in Kabylia *c.* 1845 and died in 1906, worked largely at the Gate of Talk, but was redacted by Boulifa (1904), by Mouloud Feraoun (1960), and by Mouloud Mammeri (1972)—and Mammeri's translation into French is woven into Aftersong 2. His form is the *asefrou*, a combination of three tercets on two rhymes—aab/aab/aab—with the first and third lines of each tercet having seven syllables and the second line having five.

SIX—For the six *Sedarim* ("Orders") of the Mishnah, see the entry under *seed*.

SMYRNA—invoked by Mandelstam in the octaves of "Theodosia" in his second volume of poetry, *Tristitia* (1922), and by Pindar in Fragment 82; home of the melanous merchant; early home of Hermippus of Smyrna, a third-century

B.C.E. Peripatetic, the fatuist responsible for the tale of Aeschylus's death near Gela beneath the weight of a tortoise dropped on his head by a Sicilian eagle, who had mistaken Aeschylus's baldness for a rock; birthplace of Sabbathai Zevi (1626–1676)—and there, in the autumn of 1665, he proclaimed himself publicly in the synagogue, amid the blowing of trumpets, as the expected Messiah.

SONG OF SONGS—"All the world is not worthy as the day on which the Song of Songs was given to Israel, for all the Writings are holy, but the Song of Songs is the Holy of Holies," Akiva says (*Yadayim* ["Hands"] 3:5—and elsewhere). He also said: "He who trills his voice in the chanting of the Song of Songs in banquet halls and makes it a profane song has no share in the world to come" (*Tosefta, Sanhedrin* 12:10).

SPINOZA—The three who ranted that Spinoza's lens "overlooked our rage" (Aftersong 9) have overlooked the note in Leibniz's hand (transcribed in *Leibniz, Descartes et Spinoza* by A. Foucher de Careil, Paris, 1862) in which Leibniz reports on a meeting with Spinoza after the massacre—in 1672—of the brothers De Witt: "*J'ay passé quelques heures après diner avec Spinoza; il me dit qu'il avait esté porté, le jour des massacres de MM. de Witt, de sortir la nuit et d'afficher quelque part proche du lieu (des massacres), un papier où il y aurait ultimi barbarorum. Mais son hôte luy avait fermé la maison pour l'empecher de sortir, car il se serait exposé à être déchiré.*" As for the undated Letter LVIII, from which the Maxioms draw their epigraph (rewoven into Aftersong 2)—it was addressed by Spinoza to G. H. Schuller. Also see the entries under *Sephardi* and *Joseph Del Medigo*.

STEFAN, JUDE—born in Orbec in the department of Calvados in Normandy in 1936. The poem caught in the larger web of the "Second Chant of the Hoarse Savant" appeared in *Cyprès* (1969).

SURA—One of the two principal centers of Jewish learning in Babylonia; the other was Pumbeditha. (Additional centers: Nehardea, Mechoza, Naresh, Mata Mechasya.) Despite interruptions and persecutions, these two academies continued their work for eight centuries, from the third century (Sura was founded by Rab, who was active from 219 to 247, and Pumbeditha by Judah ben Ezekiel, active from 254 to 299) to the eleventh. The participants in that work were successive generations with somewhat ambiguous chronological borders: the Amoraim (Interpreters), the Saboraim (Ponderers), and the Gaonim (see *Saadya Gaon*). Through the work of the Amoraim, the Babylonian Talmud passed from the Gate of Talk to the Gate of Text in the fifth century. That same passage *may* have been effected in Palestine in the fifth century—if one may speak of the Palestinian redaction of the Talmud as a completed piece of work. With the Talmud, which adds the Gemara—or commentary—to the already redacted Mishnah, the Oral Law received its central written formulation. See *Oral Law* and *Seed*.

*

TERCETS—To the "sharper tercets" of the Third Finding/Maxiom 12, some add a seven-stanza form of Eleazar Kalir (possibly seventh century): three words in each verset, three versets in each line, three lines in each stanza, three stanzas in each partial cycle framed by a three-verset refrain—this, twice over, with the seventh, lone stanza (see the entry under *Sabbath Queen*) completed by a three-verset refrain. Also see *Si Mohand-ou-Mhand*.

THE HOARSE SAVANT—identified by some as Alexander the Sleepless. (But see *the melanous merchant*.)

THE MELANOUS MERCHANT—identified by some as Alexander the Sleepless. (But see *the hoarse savant*.)

THE PERFECT WOMAN—See *pearls*.

THE THE—Whereas some (see Aftersong 13) point to "the the" as later sung by "one . . . who thrummed . . . of Farmington," others point to *Bouvard et Pécuchet*: "*Tiens, comme cela*, the, the, the."

THE TOTAL TABLE—Six sedentaries cite the *Shulchan Aruch* ("The Prepared Table") of Joseph Caro (1488–1575); three others cite the words of Rav Akiva on Exodus 21:1, where he likens the way in which "the judgments" are "set" to a "prepared table" (in the *Mechilta* on that passage).

THRUT—Truth is bartered for thrut (Third Finding/Maxiom 3) through the transposition of but one letter.

TORTOISISTS—One of them, José Benardete, is surely a Sephardi. See his *Infinity* (Oxford, 1964), especially pp. 51–71.

*

UNDERWOOD—typewriter used by Mandelstam in the octaves of "January 1, 1924."

*

VENUS—Analogists link the Venus of the Second Finding/Maxiom 12 (called—by some—"The Cantilena of the Oral Law") to "the full and final anagram" of "The Ayre of If" (in the Sixth Finding) by way of Galileo's enlightening anagram: "*Haec immatura à me jam frustra leguntur, o.y.*," transposable to "*Cynthiae figuras aemulatur mater amorum*" (in Kepler's *Dioptrice* of 1611). See *Del Medigo*.

VERSAL—Some cite the Nurse's prose of *Romeo and Juliet* (II, iv, 219); but others press for the verse of Butler's *Hudibras*: "Some, for brevity, / Have cast the Versal World's Nativity" (II, iii, 930).

VOWELS—See *consonants*.

*

YATAGHAN—or "ataghan," as Byron has it in *Giaour*—a dagger-like sabre with doubly curved blade. But the "yataghans of charlatans" (Gatesong Two) are not to be confused with the "yataghan of Origen" (First Finding/Maxiom 25).

*

ZENO—See *tortoisists*.

ZERACH BAR NATHAN—The Karaite savant, who corresponded with Joseph Solomon *Del Medigo* from 1620, was born in Troki, Lithuania, in 1578.

THE SCORIAE HAVE NOW BEEN GATHERED

THE SONG OF COLOPHON

Some say no arabesque
can etch, no palimpsest
can span, no portulan
can map the variants
that vex the maxioms;

for they were born to mime
the apothegm, but signs
may find the breath received
at birth is far too brief
and itch and overreach,

until the snarling lines
of long interrogation—
of text by man, and man
by text, and what is asked
when each is self-perplexed—

obsess their letters, so
distress their alphabets,
no scribe can ever will,
no colophon reveal,
their final folio,

not even if messiah
decides to send Elijah—
or patiently descends
himself—to offer us
the quiet at the end,

the gift of terminus.

CHELMAXIOMS

The Maxims • Axioms • Maxioms of Chelm

has been printed letterpress in an edition of 3500 copies,
of which 1500 copies are reserved for the Jewish Publica-
tion Society of America. It was designed, set, and printed
by Michael and Winifred Bixler. The typeface, Monotype
Van Dijck, is named after the famous seventeenth century
Dutch punchcutter and letter designer, Christoffel van
Dijck, who was an exact contemporary of Rembrandt van
Rijn and a few of whose original matrices still survive in
the great Haarlem printing house of Joh. Enschedé en
Zonen. Recut by the Monotype Corporation in 1937–38,
it is typical of the strong, graceful, and somewhat eccen-
tric type designs that prevailed in the Low Countries and
England until the time of John Baskerville. The portrait of
the author is by Barry Moser. The paper is Monadnock
Text Laid, an acid-free sheet, and the book has been
bound by the Halliday Lithograph Corporation.